316

**DARE TO**

# Make a Difference In Your School

(AND YOUR LIFE)

TO SAVE A LIFE

**OUTRECH®**

Outreach, Inc.

Vista, CA 92081

www.outreach.com

Content taken by permission from To Save a Life: Dare 2 Make Your Life Count, written by Todd Hafer and Vicki J. Kuyper in association with Snapdragon Groupsm, Tulsa, OK. Profile for Rachel Scott and Rachel's Challenge written by Elece Hollis.

ISBN: 978-1-9355-4125-7

Cover Design: Tim Downs

Interior Design: TimDowns

Printed in the United States of America

# Contents

1

Dare 2 Celebrate
the True You

Picture the cereal aisle of your local grocery store. A wall of breakfast goodness stretches out before you, box upon brightly colored box of flakes, puffs, clusters, and Os, whole grain, sugar-coated, calcium-enriched, or rainbow bright, loaded with sliced almonds, dried cranberries, yogurt bits, or marshmallow stars. Your choices for early morning nutrition are out of control.

Now switch roles. No longer the hungry consumer, you're now just a box on the shelf. Lined up with countless others, all you can do is wait for someone to pick you up and take you home. You're surrounded by choices that promise chocolaty sweetness, lower cholesterol, or a free prize inside. And you, well, you're nutritious. But that no longer feels as though it's enough.

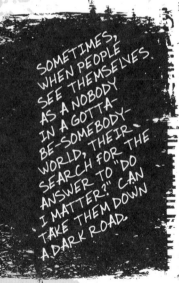

SOMETIMES, WHEN PEOPLE SEE THEMSELVES AS A NOBODY IN A GOTTA-BE-SOMEBODY WORLD, THEIR SEARCH FOR THE ANSWER TO "DO I MATTER?" CAN TAKE THEM DOWN A DARK ROAD.

There's no way to sugar-coat the truth. In a world where bigger, better, bolder, and more beautiful are considered to be not only more desirable but more valuable, it's easy to feel like a box of generic bran flakes on the cereal aisle of life. Despite what the Declaration of Independence says, it does not seem like all people are created equal. When we picture ourselves alongside those we idolize, it can feel as though we'll never measure up. We'll never be enough. Never strong enough. Never smart enough. Never thin enough. Never funny enough. Never cool enough. Never attractive enough. Never talented enough. Never enough.

Period. And that hurts.

It leaves us feeling like a product instead of a person, that last dented box of shredded wheat pushed way back on the shelf, only in demand if the rest of the aisle is bare. So, what do we do? We market ourselves. Just like cereal. If we aren't "enough" we'll become someone who is. We'll become our very own promoters. We'll advertise how desirable we are—or wish we were. At least, that's the plan, even if we're not fully aware that that's our intention.

We begin to say things we don't believe just to stand out in the crowd. We laugh at jokes we don't think are funny for the very same reason. We determine what we'll wear by how much attention our clothes—or lack thereof—will attract. We choose our friends according to what they can do for us. We join a team, a gang, or a clique because we believe others will give us more respect. We learn to flirt, swear, drink, cheat, lie, steal, or go farther than we ever intended to go. After a while, all of it feels so second nature we believe that's who we really are. Except that when we stop long enough to listen to what's going on inside, we hear that familiar whisper that says, "You're still not enough."

The funny thing is that the people we idolize, those we both envy and admire, often feel the very same way. Just look at Michael Jackson. Here was a guy with amazing talent. He stole the vocal spotlight from his older brothers at the age of five, had a record deal by the age of ten, and could dance like gravity didn't apply to him right up until the day he died. Over the course of his career, he had 13 number-one hits, received 13 Grammy awards, and sold an estimated 750 million records. His album Thriller is still the bestselling album of all time. Anyone looking from the outside in at the King of Pop would certainly consider him to be one of the "beautiful people." But obviously, Michael Jackson had trouble seeing himself that way.

No one but Jackson himself knows the true story behind the pop star's physical transformation. However, a casual glance at photos of him over the years clearly shows how Michael Jackson remade himself through plastic surgery. Apparently, even with phenomenal talent, adoring fans, and outrageous wealth there was a part of Michael Jackson that continued to whisper, "The real you still isn't good enough."

Sure, plastic surgery is extreme. But that doesn't mean it's unheard of. Even among teens. Although rhinoplasty (nose jobs) and otoplasty (ear pinnings) are the most common surgeries among those eighteen years and younger, the Society for Aesthetic Plastic Surgery says the number of girls in that same age group who've had breast augmentation has risen 500 percent over the last 10 years.

We can blame some of this pressure to look and act like a superstar on the media. Never before have we had so many people to compare ourselves with! Picture life before newspapers, magazines, movies, television, and YouTube. The only people we saw were those whose paths we crossed in real life. More than likely the people we admired were people we knew. And when we admire someone we know, we are more likely to admire them for who they really are, not for the airbrushed, agent-hyped, performance-polished image we see on TV or read about on the Internet.

But there's more to the media than celebrities. There's also advertising. Today we see more advertising in one year than people fifty years ago saw in their entire lifetimes. What does that matter? Well, an ad's job is to convince us that we need what is being sold, that we are lacking what this product or service can provide, and that without it we are not enough.

Then there is the news. Having news programs available 24 hours a day means there has to be enough "newsworthy" events going on to fill that time slot. This means stories are repeated over and over again with newscasters disclosing every detail they can dig up. This helps to blur the line between the famous and the infamous.

Sometimes, when people see themselves as a nobody in a gotta-be-somebody-world, their search for the answer to "Do I matter?" can take them down a dark road.

It happened at Columbine High School in Colorado. It's happened in Germany, Scotland, Yemen, Canada, the Netherlands, Argentina, Bosnia-Herzegovina, and Finland, as well as other states across the U.S. Teens who felt like they didn't fit in, like they were

ignored, bullied, misunderstood, unloved, or unwanted, decided to prove they mattered by taking the lives of others, sometimes along with their own. The sad fact is that those who do not believe they are significant lose sight of the fact that others are significant too.

In the movie To Save A Life, Jake ditches his longtime friend Roger in the hope of being accepted by a more popular group of friends. Roger, who already feels a bit like an outsider because of a physical handicap, becomes even more isolated as time goes by. Roger blogs, "I feel so alone, like I'm the only person in the world who feels this way, and it doesn't even matter. It's not important, maybe because I'm not important."

In a desperate attempt to prove to himself and others that he does matter, Roger brings a gun to school and threatens violence. Jake tries to reach out and help his former friend, but his words come too late. Though Roger does not harm anyone else, he takes his own life.

"Do I matter?" There are times when this question can mean the difference between life and death. Some people try to prove they do matter by committing acts of violence intended to make the world take notice. Others decide they really do not matter and take their own lives, believing their absence will have little effect on the world. The media isn't at fault when tragedies like this occur. The news, advertising, and our tendency to elevate certain people to superstar status simply aggravate a problem that already exists—the problem of not recognizing how very much each and every person matters in this world.

## BEYOND MEASURE

Millimeters, miles, cubic feet, cups, pounds, percentages, degrees, decibels ... If we're going to measure something, we need some standard to measure it against. The same is true with our self-worth. If we're trying to figure out whether or not we matter, we need to understand what kind of measure to use.

A recent survey published in Wired magazine claims that if the human body could be sold for each of its individual parts, it could be worth up to $45 million. However, when the body is simply reduced to its basic elements and minerals, it's worth only about $4.50.

Money probably isn't a very fair measuring stick since that can only measure how much our body is worth once we're no longer using it. Getting to use the body we're in right now to play video games, eat cheesecake, or listen to the number-one song on our playlist? That's priceless.

How our bodies are put together is another way we try to measure worth. In junior high and high school, it can sometimes feel like the only way. But who is to say what is attractive and what isn't? Who decides what the standard will be?

In the West African country of Mauritania, it's believed that the more you weigh, the better chance you'll have of getting a husband. On the border of Thailand and Burma, a long neck is considered attractive. Women begin their beauty treatment as young girls by stacking more and more heavy metal bands around their necks. By the time they reach adulthood, these women have weakened the muscles in their necks so much that removing the bands would cause them to suffocate. In Ethiopia scars are cut into a woman's stomach to enhance her beauty. The Maori women of New Zealand cover their lips and chins with blue tattoos.

Even in the U.S. what is considered beautiful changes with time. In the 1700s pear-shaped hips were considered attractive. (So was shaving your eyebrows and replacing them with ones made of press-on mouse skin!) In the 1800s women were encouraged to look frail and pale. In the 1920s women bound their chests to have more boyish figures.

Though a guy's physical appearance doesn't seem to be under the magnifying glass quite as often as a girl's, that doesn't mean there isn't pressure to have a rock star or sports star physique. But what if you were born with more of a Homer Simpson silhouette? Sure, you can work out, eat right, and, if you care to, follow the latest trends in fashion. But you can only work with what you were born with. And you were born with something no one else in the history of the world was given: your unique body—not to mention your one-of-a-kind personality and life story!

When it comes to measuring worth, one standard seems to always hold true. The rarer something is, the more value it has. A one-of-a-kind item is as rare as you can get. Even if you happen to be born an identical twin, you know (probably better than anyone else!) that you're still one-of-a-kind. You may look alike, but that doesn't mean you're the same. There isn't any one, nor has there ever been any one, nor will there ever be any one exactly like you.

Each person is like a single piece in a giant jigsaw puzzle that stretches through time. We're all different shapes and colors, each filling a unique spot that helps complete the final picture. You may be an eye-catching flower petal on a begonia, a burst of lava from an erupting volcano, or a razor-sharp tooth on a Bengal tiger. Or you may be one of those blue pieces of sky. You know, the ones that at first glance all seem to look alike. But try and put one piece of sky into the spot designed for another piece and what happens? It won't fit.

You can try jamming it in, pounding it down, or bending the corners up a bit. But even if you succeed in cramming that piece into a spot where it doesn't belong, it will never look quite right. And somewhere else in the puzzle there will be a hole in the picture—a spot where that piece would have fit just perfectly.

Every piece plays its part. But sometimes it takes awhile to

> ## NO MAN WAS EVER GREAT BY IMITATION. 
> -Samuel Johnson

find your spot. That's part of the adventure of being a teen. You're discovering who you are and where you fit—what part of the big picture you were created to fill. That process involves trial and error, just like working any puzzle with a couple billion pieces! That means you can feel free to try out for the soccer team, see if playing drums is your thing, or join the chess club with your head held high. You can feel equally proud of being a bookworm, a computer geek, or a skater. As a matter of fact, you may discover you have a knack for being all three.

If you're searching for a standard by which to measure yourself, forget about measuring yourself against others. Every time you compare yourself with another piece of the puzzle, or try to change yourself from a lava flow to a tiger tooth because stripes are totally in this season, you lose sight of how truly valuable that one-of-a-kind you really is. You lose sight of your true worth.

It's like comparing apples to oranges or blue sky to begonias. Comparing yourself with other people doesn't prove a thing, except that we are all different. Unique. That's a given. Instead, compare who you are trying to be with who you were created to be. That's a standard that will remain constant. No one can ever be a better you than you. And that's something worth celebrating.

## LET THE CELEBRATION BEGIN!

So, let's get back to those three questions that sum up the search for significance.

Do I matter? Without a doubt. Regardless of your GPA, the size or brand on the label of your jeans, or how many friends you have on Facebook, you have a unique place in the world—a place no one but you can fill. Without you, history would be incomplete, like a jigsaw puzzle missing a vital piece. You are a one-of-a-kind, irreplaceable, incomparable treasure.

Why am I here? You're still in the process of figuring that out. The more you get to know yourself—your strengths and weaknesses, hopes and dreams, talents and gifts—the more you'll understand about where you fit in the big picture of life.

Am I loved? Whoa. That's a whole other story. But right now we're going to look at a loyal sidekick of love. It's called acceptance.

Every individual matters in this world, but that doesn't mean every individual is accepted by others. This isn't news to you or to us. We've all felt the sting of rejection. It's what fuels those "never good enough" feelings we battle inside.

At one time or another in our performance-driven, appearance-obsessed, status-seeking culture, we've all been judged by others. And if we're honest, we know we've plopped ourselves down in that judge's seat more than a time or two. We can't force others to accept us. However, we can do something to step down from that judge's seat and help to fight that inner battle of insecurity that erupts when others refuse to see us for who we truly are. The very best thing we can do is learn to accept ourselves.

COMPARING YOURSELF WITH OTHER PEOPLE DOESN'T PROVE A THING, EXCEPT THAT WE ARE ALL DIFFERENT.

We can see you rolling your eyes from here. The term "self-acceptance" often gets a bad rap. That's because it sounds like the consolation prize for those who don't come in first. You've got to learn to accept your limitations and be thankful for what you've got, right? Nothing could be further from the truth.

Consider Wilma Rudolph. From birth it seemed as though "Willie" had more than her fair share of tough breaks. She was the 20th of 22 children born into an African-American family in Tennessee. Known as "the sickliest child in Clarksville," Willie suffered through measles, mumps, chicken pox, double pneumonia, and scarlet fever. At the age of four, she contracted polio, which left her left leg paralyzed. At five, Willie began wearing a metal leg brace. Her poor health prevented her from attending kindergarten or first grade, so she began school in the second grade. In her autobiography, Willie explained that she attended a segregated school, but her red hair and light skin, along with her leg brace, made her feel like an outsider among her peers.

Willie's father was a railroad porter, and her mother worked as a maid. Even with a grueling work schedule and a large family, Willie's parents and siblings faithfully helped her strengthen her weak leg with physical therapy four times a day, three to four days a week. One Sunday at church, when Willie was 11 years old, she removed her brace and proudly walked unassisted down the center aisle.

At 13, Willie got involved in organized sports at school. Like her sister Yolanda, Willie joined the basketball team. But Willie sat on the sidelines for three years, not once being called in to play a game. When Willie finally made it onto the court, she was spotted by a college coach who invited her to attend a summer sports camp. There Willie tried running track.

Soon Willie was not only running, but winning, every race she ran. At the age of twenty "the sickliest child in Clarksville" became known as "the fastest woman alive." In the 1960 Olympic games, Willie won the 100-meter dash, the 200-meter dash, and the 400-meter relay. She became the first American woman to win three gold medals during a single Olympics, matching the accomplishment of her personal hero, Olympic runner Jesse Owens.

When Willie returned home to Clarksville, the city proposed a parade in her honor—a racially segregated parade—but Willie refused to participate unless everyone, regardless of race, could take part. Her hometown celebration became the city's first racially integrated event.

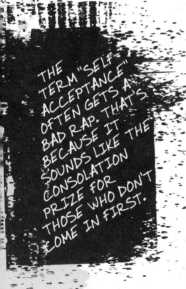

THE TERM "SELF-ACCEPTANCE" OFTEN GETS A BAD RAP. THAT'S BECAUSE IT SOUNDS LIKE THE CONSOLATION PRIZE FOR THOSE WHO DON'T COME IN FIRST.

Willie said she believed God had greater things for her to do than win medals, and she was right. The fastest woman alive retired from running in 1962 and became a second grade teacher and high school coach. Later she founded the Wilma Rudolph Foundation to help disadvantaged young athletes discover their true potential. She also traveled with Billy Graham and the Baptist Christian Athletes, inspiring people all over the world with her story.

"But wait!" you say. "Foul! Wilma Rudolph was just another winner. She did come in first! She was one of those people who comes out on top, someone others celebrate. Not everyone who wants to walk will walk. Not everyone who trains hard will win an Olympic gold medal."

That's true. But it's not Willie's medals that are the most important part of her story. They simply brought her amazing life to the attention of the world. Back when Willie was a kid, her goal wasn't to win a medal and become an Olympic legend. As a matter of fact, Willie never even heard of the Olympics until she was 16. Long before she began running, Willie's goal was simple—to see if she could walk. This was something doctors said she might never be able to do. Yet Willie reached her goal, literally, one step at a time. And she wound up with Olympic gold thrown in for good measure.

Willie's true competition wasn't other runners. She was competing against herself. When it came to self-acceptance, she had a choice: resignation or celebration. She chose celebration. Willie saw beyond who she was at the moment to who she believed she could be—who she believed God had created her to be. Then she did what she could to help herself go and grow in that direction.

Just like Willie, your life story is written one day at a time. You may be facing tough challenges. You may struggle with disadvantages, disabilities, or discouragement. You may not have the support of a family cheering you on like Willie did when she was young. But you're not alone. There's Someone pulling for you. Someone who knows you inside and out. Someone who understands your place in the big picture and knows exactly where the puzzle piece that is "you" belongs. He wants to help you see yourself through His eyes. He wants you to know you're so much more than "enough."

## POETRY IN MOTION

No one knows a piece of art better than the artist who created it. Only an artist can tell us why he chose oil paint over watercolor or why she decided to sculpt a rabbit munching on a Game Boy instead of a carrot. Only the artist knows when his or her masterpiece is complete. The same is true of the Artist who created you.

In your search for significance, nothing can help you understand and accept yourself more fully than getting to know the Artist behind the masterpiece that is you. One quick glance at the world around us confirms that we live in the ultimate art gallery: the Grand Canyon, the Rocky Mountains, tide pools, thunderstorms, sunsets, kangaroos, and kinkajous. The creativity and complexity of nature outshines anything found on the walls and in the halls of any museum.

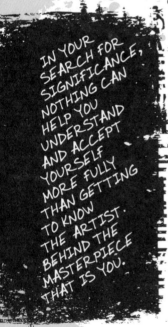

IN YOUR SEARCH FOR SIGNIFICANCE, NOTHING CAN HELP YOU UNDERSTAND AND ACCEPT YOURSELF MORE FULLY THAN GETTING TO KNOW THE ARTIST BEHIND THE MASTERPIECE THAT IS YOU.

But even more impressive than the rings of Saturn or the funky glow-in-the-dark fish that live miles beneath the surface of the sea is the people "art" all around us. We've mentioned before that there are about 6.5 billion people alive right now. If we're talking numbers, your body has about 100 billion neurons and between 50 and 100 trillion cells. That's complex!

Some people believe that life just happened, that people are a product of chance, not art. That's like saying Michelangelo's

> **JESUS ACCEPTS YOU THE WAY YOU ARE BUT LOVES YOU TOO MUCH TO LEAVE YOU THAT WAY.**
> -Lee Venden

statue of David "just happened." Regardless of how much time passed, it would be hard to believe that a common hunk of marble— without any help from an outside hand—could wind up looking like a hunky teenager holding a slingshot. But even that would be more likely than something as complex as life just starting on its own.

Imagine what you'd think if you saw that statue of David take its first breath. If David got down off his pedestal and took a stroll through the streets of Florence, wouldn't you agree that would be nothing short of a miracle? Is it any less a miracle that a bunch of carbon and oxygen got organized enough on its own to play the piano, understand calculus, or fall in love? How about become a living, breathing human being?

Believing in God, the Artist who created this incredible world with an almighty hand, takes faith. After all, we can't see Him, hug Him, or hear His voice on a cell phone. But believing that this world and the unique individuals who live in it are nothing more than a glitch, something that grew out of nothing to become living works of art, takes faith too—faith that people are no more than those basic elements and minerals we mentioned before, and that we truly are worth only about four-and-a-half bucks each.

In Psalm 139, verses 13 through 16, you will learn that the Bible has a lot to say about you, God's amazing creation: "You made my whole being; you formed me in my mother's body. I praise you because you made me in an amazing and wonderful way. What you have done is wonderful. I know this very well. You saw my bones being formed as I took shape in my mother's body. When I was put together there, you saw my body as it was formed. All the days planned for me were written in your book before I was one day old" (NCV).

You are a living poem. Some people are sonnets. Some are limericks. Some are haiku. But each person is a unique work of art. As a living poem, you are being written one day at a time, as both you and God hold the pen. God created you and has a wonderful plan for you. However, you play a part in deciding what message your poem will ultimately convey.

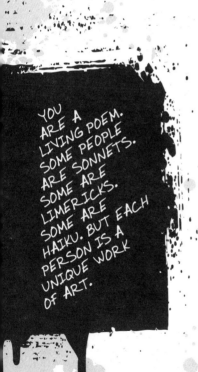

YOU ARE A LIVING POEM. SOME PEOPLE ARE SONNETS. SOME ARE LIMERICKS. SOME ARE HAIKU. BUT EACH PERSON IS A UNIQUE WORK OF ART.

A poem is just a song in need of a tune. You can write your life like Wilma Rudolph, taking what some people feel is a lament and turning it into a victory song. Or you may choose to write your life more along the lines of a country tune, crying over what you've lost, how hard life is, and how you're never going to amount to anything. If you go with Plan B, don't be surprised to find a lot of rejection along the way. You can't expect others to do something you refuse to do—accept yourself.

But suppose you go with Plan A. Suppose you

take an honest look at who you are today.

refuse to market yourself by pretending to be someone you're not.

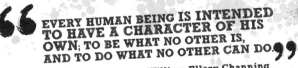

> **EVERY HUMAN BEING IS INTENDED TO HAVE A CHARACTER OF HIS OWN; TO BE WHAT NO OTHER IS, AND TO DO WHAT NO OTHER CAN DO.**
>
> -William Ellery Channing

consider what the Artist who created you says about His creation.

choose celebration over resignation when it comes to self-acceptance.

If you do these four things, your life will have a better chance of becoming a song you'll sing loud and proud. Not only that, you may soon find others singing along with you. When you're honest about who you really are, others will feel more at ease being themselves around you, which will make you feel more at ease ... and on and on it goes.

Self-acceptance is more than a gift you give yourself. It's the first step you need to take if you want to reach out to those around you. If you want to find out what love is all about.

# DID YOU KNOW?

**1.** You are a superstar.

—Philippians 2:15-16

**2.** You are rich.

—1 Timothy 6:6

**3.** God has great plans for you.

—Jeremiah 29:11

**4.** God remembers every one of your tears.

—Psalm 56:8

**5.** You make God sing.

—Zephaniah 3:17

# 2

## Dare 2 Give, Dare to Share

"Mommy, won't his feet be cold?" Four-year-old Hannah stared at the man's bare toes peeking through his well-worn shoes.

"His shoes will keep him warm." Hannah's mother didn't know what else to say. The line for Thanksgiving dinner at the rescue mission was long and there was no way she could do anything about this one man right now. Both she and Hannah needed to keep doing their part to serve meals, to keep the line moving.

Hannah looked down at her own warm pink socks. "Mommy, he can have my socks."

Talk about putting yourself in someone else's shoes.

Hannah saw a need and wanted to meet it. She was willing to suffer cold feet so a stranger's feet could be warm. Although her tiny pink socks weren't big enough to help out a stranger that day, the next morning, Hannah's mother took her daughter to purchase 100 pairs of new socks to donate to the shelter. But they didn't stop there.

Hannah and her parents founded a nonprofit organization called Hannah's Socks. Over the last five years, they've provided more than 45,000 pairs of new socks to shelters in Ohio. And they're just getting started.

Four-year-olds are not usually known for their empathy and generosity. The words "mine" and "no" come more readily to mind. But Hannah grew up in a generous home, one where caring and sharing were modeled. Her father, Vic, writes on the Hannah's Socks Web site, "'It is better to give than to receive.' Most of us have heard those words, recorded in the Bible from the lips of Jesus. They express one of the central tenets of authentic Christian faith: generosity."

A "tenet" is just a fancy word for a belief or teaching. As for "authentic," you know what that is. It's what we all want to be. Real, 100 percent genuine—no fillers or additives. The uniquely original people God created each one of us to be. So, living our

faith in an authentic, no-room-for-faking-it way means generosity should come as naturally to us as it did to Hannah that Thanksgiving Day.

For many of us, Thanksgiving comes every day of the year. Our closets overflow with outfit options. Our kitchens are so well stocked we can even snack between meals. We have our very own bed to sleep in at night. We have so much to take care of we often can't even find what we're looking for. We have so many reasons each and every day to say, "Thank You, God!"

We have so much to give and so many reasons to share. So, what's stopping us?

## LIVING LARGE

We live in a "me first" world. Get ahead. Be first in line. Have it your way. Not that it's bad to share. Just make sure your own needs are taken care of first. After that, you're free to give away what's left. That Willy Wonka tee from Uncle Sid. The glitter mascara that came free with a bottle of facial scrub. Those jars of pickled beets and cans of creamed corn that have been hiding for who-knows-how-long in the pantry behind the bags of your favorite chips. Box it up and drop it off. Your good deed's done without ever having to get too close to anyone who might actually be in need.

Once it's over, you feel pretty good. No, not just good, you feel downright proud. Not only have you cleaned out your closet to make room for more, you've actually changed the life of some poor, unfortunate soul. You didn't have to do it, but you did. That was nice of you. More than nice, that was good. You are a good person.

Now, don't get us wrong. Donating stuff you no longer need to others who can use it is a good thing. A really good thing. But generosity is not about how much we give. It's about how much we love. Chapter 13 in Paul's first letter to the Corinthians has been nicknamed the Bible's "Love Chapter." It says that if we give everything we have to the poor—everything—but do not do it with love, it's the same as if we've given nothing at all.

St. Vincent de Paul, the guy all of those thrift stores were named after, was a French priest who worked hard to take care of the poor back in the 1600s. He said, "It is only because of your love, only your love, that the poor will for-give you the bread you give them."

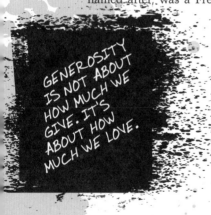

GENEROSITY IS NOT ABOUT HOW MUCH WE GIVE. IT'S ABOUT HOW MUCH WE LOVE.

It isn't easy to be on the receiving end of a gift you can't return. It can humble you. Make you feel small. Embarrassed. But if a gift comes wrapped in love, rather than pity, obligation, or a giver's own need to look good, it can help the one who receives it feel cared for. Noticed. Valued. Significant.

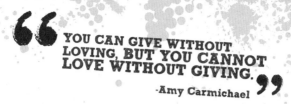

That's not all. When you give out of love, you actually do yourself a favor. You wind up with more, not less. Remember, Jesus said it is better or "more blessed" to give than receive. More blessed. More.

The book of Proverbs in the Old Testament says, "The world of the generous gets larger and larger; the world of the stingy gets smaller and smaller. The one who blesses others is abundantly blessed; those who help others are helped" (11:24–25 MSG).

If you live a life focused only on yourself, you'll find yourself living in a very small world—a world where love is measured out in tiny doses, like cold medicine. You may share a teaspoon here or a few drops there, as long as it's convenient and comfortable and doesn't deplete the stash you're storing up for yourself. Just in case you need it.

But love can't be stored. It can't be hoarded or saved for a rainy day. Love isn't really love until it's given away.

In your search for significance, if the answer to "Am I loved?" is "Yes," then you have something to give: love. Just how you choose to share that love is where the fun comes in.

## "LITTLE" IS THE NEW "BIG"

There's a penny on the sidewalk. Do you stoop down to pick it up? That depends on how much it's worth to you. If you're feeling rich, why bother? What's it going to get you? A stick of gum? Not even.

But what if your pockets are empty? What if you haven't eaten since yesterday? In that case, a penny may seem like the beginning of something big.

Jesus had great things to say about a widow who gave a gift of two pennies. She wasn't the only one donating money at the temple that day. There were lots of people, rich people, dropping off fat wads of Benjamins or Caesars or whoever's face happened to be on the money at that time. But Jesus told His disciples this woman had given the biggest gift of the day. Talk about math-challenged. At least, that's what Jesus' friends must have thought. Then Jesus explained that the other people had given a tiny portion of what they had. This woman had given everything, 100 percent of her financial holdings. They had given in part, while she had given all.

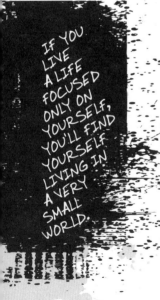

IF YOU LIVE A LIFE FOCUSED ONLY ON YOURSELF, YOU'LL FIND YOURSELF LIVING IN A VERY SMALL WORLD.

You may feel as though you don't have a lot to give. Especially right now. You're not even a bona fide adult yet. Okay, so you do have love. But, what do you do with it? Do you have to start a whole nonprofit organization, like Hannah and her parents, to make a difference? If you just give your two cents, does it really count?

It does if you're the one who needs those two cents.

And it does if you give those two cents because you want to, not because you feel like you should.

In the New Testament the apostle Paul writes, "You must each decide in your own heart how much to give. And don't give reluctantly or in response to pressure. 'For God loves a person who gives cheerfully'" (2 Corinthians 9:7 NLT).

Did you get that? God prizes cheerful givers. Cheerful givers are those who are happily willing to share what they have. They may not be the biggest givers or the ones who inspire the largest following. They may not get their faces plastered across the evening news. Cheerful givers are often known as "anonymous." That's because they're more concerned with shining a spotlight on others' needs than on themselves.

What can you cheerfully give right here, right now?

If you're unsure of where to start, Jesus shares a tip for beginners in Matthew 10:40–42: "It's best to start small. Give a cool cup of water to someone who is thirsty, for instance. The smallest act of giving or receiving makes you a true apprentice" (MSG).

Sounds doable, right? Give a cup of cool water. An encouraging word. A smile. A moment of your time. Maybe even a pair of socks. Preferably clean.

## WHAT HAVE YOU GOT TO GIVE?

Seeing needs is one thing. Seeing what you've got to give is quite another. Cheerful givers need 20/20 vision in both. That means it's time to check yourself out. No, step away from the mirror. What you need to check out are four areas of your life: your stuff (what you have on hand), your talents, your experience, and your passion.

If we were into nerdy little acronyms, we'd note that this spells STEP. But since we're not, we'll just mention that knowing these four things can help you take a big STEP forward toward becoming a cheerful giver.

Fourteen-year-old Kaylee Marie Radzyminski didn't realize how truly valuable the stuff she owned could be until she spoke with troops returning from military duty overseas. "What did you miss most?" she asked returning soldiers. Their number-one answer was no big surprise: family. But over and over again, the men and women she talked to mentioned "entertainment" as number two.

That got Kaylee thinking. She started boxing up some of her own CDs and DVDs and encouraged friends and classmates to do the same. Then she shipped what they'd collected overseas.

That was the beginning of Tunes 4 the Troops. Since 2005, Kaylee has helped send more than 600,000 CDs, DVDs, and books on CD to troops in Iraq, Afghanistan, and Kuwait. That's more than $10 million worth of entertainment. Kaylee saw a need. Then she saw how what she already had could fill that need. Just like Hannah and her socks.

WHAT DOES YOUR TRUE TREASURE LOOK LIKE? DOES IT HAVE A FACE OR A PRICE TAG?

Admit it. You've probably got stuff. Most of us do. Stuff that could make someone else's life a little easier, happier, or healthier. Stuff that you could share or give away. It doesn't matter if you've got a lot or a little. What matters is that if you see a need, and God brings that stuff to mind and says "share," you can let it go.

A funny thing happens when you loosen your death grip on the stuff you own. You find you can live with a lot less—and still be happy. A 20-something friend of Vicki's recently returned from working with the Peace Corps. Caitlin lived with a tribe in a remote part of Zambia for two years. There she educated the people about AIDS, learned a new language, battled snakes, and was adopted as an honorary daughter by the chief of the tribe.

Caitlin lived in a simple hut. No electricity. No running water. No walk-in closet. No big screen, or even tiny screen, TV. Her bathroom was in a separate hut outside her door. Well, it was until she accidentally burned it to the ground one night when she set the roof on fire with her candle.

When asked how living in Zambia had changed her, Caitlin said she realized how little she really needed to be content. But the longer she's back in the States, the more Caitlin says she winds up visiting the mall with her friends—and the more she feels that urge to buy something. Just because. First it was that tug of "I want that." Then she said it felt more like "I need that." Caitlin said she doesn't want to slip back into filling her life with stuff, but it isn't easy. Here, shopping is entertainment.

If you love to shop or simply enjoy watching your stash of video games grow and overflow, ask yourself what it would take for you to willingly part with some of your favorite things. Jesus said, "Where your treasure is, there your heart will be also" (Luke 12:34). What does your true treasure look like? Does it have a face or a price tag?

You don't have to give away everything you own and live in a hut to love well. Generosity is like a bicep. The more you stretch it and work it out, the bigger and stronger it gets. Remember to start small. Give a cup of cool water.

Or maybe a cool CD to Tunes 4 the Troops.

## DON'T JUST DISPLAY YOUR TALENT, GIVE IT AWAY

So, America's got stuff. Lots of it. It's piled up in malls, packed away in storage bins, and then sold on eBay so someone new can take care of it for a while. But according to TV, America's got talent too—along with the rest of the world. But what we see on TV is a pretty limited picture of what talent looks like: acting, singing, dancing, playing sports, juggling flaming guitars, catching chickens while twanging out a country tune.

Talent also grows in much quieter, less showy varieties, like teaching, encouraging, or being able to counsel others with wise advice. Some people are naturally gifted at working with people. Others are more comfortable with hands-on skills like fixing cars, programming computers, or balancing a budget. Do you know where your talent lies?

You've got talent. Everyone does. That's part of God's wonderful design for us all. Whether this talent is something you were born with or a skill you've acquired over time, you can use it to do more than earn a living or entertain your friends. You can use it to help someone in need.

When Isabelle Redford was five, her parents went on a missionary trip to Haiti. When they came back, they told their daughter about twin girls they'd met whose mother had died. Isabelle's immediate response was, "What can we do? We have to help!" At such a young age, the only thing Isabelle was certain she could do was draw. It was something she'd loved as far back as she could remember. So, Isabelle

> **IT IS NOT THE MAGNITUDE OF OUR ACTIONS BUT THE AMOUNT OF LOVE THAT IS PUT INTO THEM THAT MATTERS.**
>
> -Mother Teresa

decided to start making greeting cards and selling them at garage sales.

Her goal was to raise $5,000 to build a home for these girls in Haiti. Over the past two years, she's sold her cards not only at garage sales but through the Global Orphan Project. Through her artwork, Isabelle has raised more than $10,000. That was enough money to build the Isabelle Redford House of Hope in Haiti—and to break ground for another orphanage in Malawi, Africa.

Being five like Isabelle, or four like Hannah, has its advantages. At that age, you don't worry about what other people will think. You don't stress over all the things that could stand in your way. You don't think, "This week is totally booked. There's no way I have time."

You think of simple things. "I can draw." "I can give my socks." And so you do it.

What comes easily to you? What do other people tell you you're good at? What do you really enjoy? How can you use these gifts and talents to meet the needs of those around you?

Think of simple things like:

I can cook up a mean burger at a homeless shelter.

I can read my favorite kids' book at an after-school program.

I can swing a hammer to help build a home for someone in need.

I can play piano at a retirement home.

I can write a note to someone who could use an encouraging word.

I can play video games for charity. (Yup, you read that right.)

"We heard about this great charity, Child's Play, that gives toys and games to hospitals for sick kids to play with, but we didn't know how we wanted to raise money for it," says Michael Mays, one of a group of four teens from Rose Hill, Kansas. "We didn't really have any typical 'money raising' skills."

But Michael and his friends, Dylan Waller, Dalton Plummer, and Michael Whinery, were all downright awesome at playing video games. So they decided to have a 72-hour video game marathon streamed via webcam and promoted through online chats, where they could encourage people to donate to Child's Play.

Their first marathon raised $257. With the hope of raising more money in the future, they created the group "Marathons Avast!" Their mission statement is: "To overheat consoles, help charities, and play video games. We pride ourselves on not only quality gaming, but an overall fun and entertaining atmosphere with an emphasis on humor, because that's how we roll."

WE DON'T NEED TO KEEP RELIVING HARD TIMES. BUT WE CAN RECYCLE THOSE HARD TIMES IN WAYS THAT HELP OTHERS HEAL.

Even making people laugh is a talent you can give away in a creative way. But caring and sharing is not always video marathons and laugh fests. Sometimes God may ask you to share something you wished you'd never received in the first place.

## RECYCLING THE HARD TIMES

When you're six years old, toys are a big deal. So when Ashlee Smith's toys were destroyed in a house fire in 2005, it was something she wouldn't soon forget. Two years later, when an illegal campfire started a blaze that destroyed 254 homes in the Angora Ridge Fire, Ashlee's own experience came rushing back. She thought of all the kids in Lake Tahoe, California, whose homes had burned down. She knew what they were feeling. And she knew how to help.

Ashlee began collecting toys to give to kids who'd lost everything they owned in the fire. "I wanted to help the little victims in a big way," she said. But even after the fire was extinguished, Ashlee kept on going. Today "Ashlee's Toy Closet" and its now ten-year-old founder continue to provide toys, books, and clothing to children affected by disasters.

Ashlee turned something that hurt into something that helped. She took her own painful experience and used what she learned from it to comfort others. That's exactly what the Bible says God will help each one of us do. Second Corinthians 1:4 says, "He comes alongside us when we go through hard times, and before you know it, he brings us alongside someone else who is going through hard times so that we can be there for that person just as God was there for us" (MSG).

We don't need to keep reliving hard times. God wants to help us heal the hole in our souls. But we can recycle those hard times in ways that help others heal. Our most painful experiences can become wise teachers. They can give us insight into how people are feeling and what they may need when faced with a similar situation.

Have you, or someone close to you, fought a battle with cancer, depression, diabetes, asthma, or any other serious physical or mental illness?

Have you been the victim of divorce, violence, prejudice, rape, or abuse?

Have you, like Ashlee, suffered the effects of a disaster?

Experiences like these cry out for comfort. One day, because of what you've learned from your own painful experience, you may find you have exactly what it takes to answer someone else's cry.

Maybe you'll volunteer to answer phones on a hotline, raise money for a cure, or simply drop someone a note that says, "I've been there. If you ever need to talk, I'm here to listen."

It won't always be easy. It may stir up things you'd rather forget. But remember when Jesus said, "It's more blessed to give than receive"? Helping others heal has a way of helping us heal. It helps us take our eyes off of our own problems for a while and gives our hearts a good workout. It helps our love, empathy, and generosity get up and grow.

## STARTING A CHAIN REACTION

Rachel Joy Scott was a fun-loving girl who loved the colors yellow and lavender and the movie, Titanic. She was a real girl from a real family, not so different from other girls her age. Rachel loved to write and her journals are full of her feelings, and her dreams and hopes.

It's easy to see that she suffered the insecurities and trials common to most teens. At times she felt lonely, afraid, angry, and frustrated with school, family, and life in general.

She struggled with peer pressure and fought to stand by her convictions, but she was determined to be a good and kind person, love her parents, and reach out to those who were hurting or different from her. Her journals reveal that she desired to stand out in the crowd, shun mediocrity, and have a life that counted.

When she was 13, she drew an outline of her hands on the back of her dresser with these words: "These hands belong to Rachel Joy Scott and will someday touch millions of people's hearts." Later, she wrote a paper for school titled, "My Ethics, My Codes of Life". In it she wrote, "My biggest aspects of ethics include being honest, compassionate, and looking for the best and beauty in everyone...Compassion is the greatest form of love humans have to offer...My definition of compassion is forgiving, loving, helping, leading, and showing mercy for others. I have this theory that if one person can go out of their way to show compassion, then it will start a chain reaction of the same. People will never know how far a little kindness can go."

This uncommon vision to touch millions with kindness and compassion seemed unfulfilled when Rachel Scott was the first person killed at Columbine High School in the tragic school shootings on April 20, 1999. But that is not the end of her story or her impact. Her code and the message of her life became the basis for a non-profit organization called Rachel's Challenge, established by her father, Darrell Scott, in her memory.

Its mission is to inspire, equip, and empower every person to create a permanent positive culture change in his or her school, business, and community by starting a chain reaction of kindness and compassion. Rachel's acts of kindness and compassion coupled with the contents of her six diaries have become the foundation for one of the most life-changing school programs in America. The organization uses Rachel's life story and the circumstances of the Columbine tragedy to quell bullying, violence, and suicides among students. "Friends of Rachel" clubs in schools are intended to sustain long-term results.

Rachel Joy Scott wasn't perfect, but she was extraordinary, someone to look up to, someone who could see things from an eternal perspective. She worked to be a good friend and encourage kindness and understanding. Rachel's life, though it ended tragically, continues to change the world. More than 13 million people have heard Rachel's story since she died. Her voice continues to speak to young people everywhere that our convictions must wear shoes and love in action can truly change the world.

Part of Rachel's legacy is to show you that you don't have to be a super-teen to make a difference in the lives of those around you. It will take courage, commitment, and a caring heart to stand up for what's right and reach out in a positive way to others, but if Rachel could do it, so can you. That's what she's saying even now.

## A PASSION FOR CHANGE

Zach Hunter doesn't have a natural talent for speaking. In fact, for years Zach suffered from an anxiety disorder that left him feeling nauseous and paranoid at the thought of standing up and speaking in front of a group of people. But by the time he was 16, Zach had spoken to more

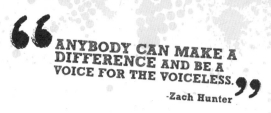

> **"ANYBODY CAN MAKE A DIFFERENCE AND BE A VOICE FOR THE VOICELESS."**
>
> -Zach Hunter

than half a million people at live events, appeared on national television, and even delivered a speech at the White House—all to help bring an end to modern-day slavery.

That takes courage and passion, two things Zach seems to have an abundance of. But it wasn't always that way. Zach's passion to fight injustice began during Black History Month when Zach was in seventh grade. His courage began the minute he decided to do something about what he had learned.

As Zach studied the lives of Frederick Douglass and Harriet Tubman, he commented to his mom that if he'd lived back then, he would have done something to abolish slavery. She told him that slavery was as much a reality today as it had ever been. "I had all of these emotions about it and I wasn't sure what to think about the idea of having modern slavery," Zach says, "but I didn't think it was enough just to have emotions."

So, Zach launched Loose Change to Loosen Chains. According to Real Simple magazine, almost $10.5 billion of loose change is just hanging out in the couch cushions and jelly jars of American households. Zach found about $200 in his own home. Then he invited his school and church to get involved. They collected about $8,500 in change, which was donated to abolitionist organizations such as Free the Slaves and International Justice Mission.

Since then, Zach has continued to change the world with change. He's also written three books, including his latest: Lose Your Cool: Discovering a Passion That Changes You and the World. You can check out his new Web site at www.zach-hunter.me.

Zach's passion is to end slavery in his lifetime. Is there a passion stirring in you?

Listen. You may hear a whisper that says, "I've got to do something" about social issues such as modern-day slavery, world hunger, or child prostitution. Maybe a passion is sparked by something you read online or heard on the news. Maybe it's tied to a very public need or cause in your school, church, or community. Or maybe it's as private and personal as finding out the family of a friend has lost their home and is now living in their car.

If you hear that whisper—the one that says, "I've got to do something"—take time to listen. And pray. Prayer is one way to give, one way to care. But don't stop there if you feel God is calling you to act. Do something. No act of love is too small. Even a cup of cool water counts. Just ask Jesus.

Sharing one small gift of kindness makes a difference. It's a great start. But the more often you give, the more you'll find you feel like giving. And that's a good thing for both you and those around you. Generosity takes you down roads you might never before have considered traveling. Roads that can open your eyes to things like modern-day slavery, troops overseas, or one homeless person's cold feet. Roads that can open your heart to what loving others in a practical, sacrificial way really looks like.

Of course, there are lots of people in this world who help others and are generous with their resources. These people do good things because they have learned that it feels good, and they sense that it's the right thing to do. They're right. Their actions will bring them satisfaction. There is another reason we do all we can for others, however. When we think about all that God has given us, when we acknowledge the good He has done in our lives, we desire to be kind and generous to others just because we know it pleases Him. Our hearts are filled with gratitude that calls us to follow His example and honor His wishes. We love because He loved; we give because He gave; we show compassion because He showed compassion; we share because He shared, and that makes our actions even more significant. It makes them divinely inspired.

As generosity expands your view of the world and the size of your heart, it can also help you discover more about who God created you to be. Who knows, there may be an abolitionist, fundraiser, entrepreneur, performer, caregiver, author, or public speaker in you just waiting for the right time to shine.

## FIND OUT MORE

If you'd like to find out how you can help with any of the charities mentioned in this chapter, you can find out more by visiting their Web sites:

www.hannassocks.org

www.tunes4thetroops.org

www.theglobalorphanproject.org

www.childsplaycharity.org

www.ashleestoycloset.org

www.rachelschallenge.org

www.freetheslaves.net

www.ijm.org (International Justice Mission)

CHAPTER 2

# DID YOU KNOW?

- When it comes to volunteering to support charitable causes, American teens are the best. Consider these numbers released by major charities like World Vision, Habitat for Humanity, and Northwest Harvest:

- More American teens volunteer for charity work (56 percent) than adults (46 percent).

- More American teens volunteer for charity work (56 percent) than work at part-time jobs (39 percent).

- Parents and guardians said that 82 percent of their teens regularly do something to support charitable causes: donating money, wearing a button, recruiting, and fundraising.

- A Harris Interactive survey says that teens have become 25 percent more involved in volunteering for charitable organizations, even though the economic downturn has led to cuts in allowances and more teens holding full-time job

# 3

Dare 2 Redefine

Cool

"This could be one of the happiest moments of my life--if only I could delete that mental picture of the girl collapsed on the track..."

They stood atop the awards podium, admiring their gleaming gold state championship medals, basking in the adoration of a crowd of 15,000 cheering track fans. As they tried to drink it all in, the Maranatha Academy 4 X 800-meter relay team wondered if they were dreaming. Coming into the 2009 Kansas State Track and Field Meet, the lady Eagles weren't even seeded among the top six relay teams. But, as they had learned as students at a Christian high school, God works in mysterious ways.

The Eagles got off to a flying start in their race, and by the time the first two runners had completed their two laps, it was clear the Maranatha school record was toast. But a gold medal? That was off the table. The Panthers from Pittsburg-St. Mary's had a commanding 20-meter lead on the field, and the team from Olpe seemed to have second place locked down. Still, a school record and a quartet of bronze medals sounded pretty good to Ali Bailey, Bethany Zarda, Mallory Keith, and Christa Courtney--a team that hadn't even figured to be in the mix.

Then, in a matter of seconds, the Eagles saw bronze transform into gold.

As she charged into the homestretch, the Panthers' third runner, Emmalia White, collapsed on the track, succumbing to the punishing pace she set for herself in the sticky Kansas heat. White went down like a pair of fists, but this was the state meet, and the championship was at stake. She peeled herself off the track and lurched toward the exchange zone, where anchor leg Faith Miller was urging her on. When White approached the zone, Miller started jogging forward, her extended hand ready to receive the baton handoff they'd practiced dozens of times.

But when Miller looked back to check on White's progress, she saw her teammate crumple to the track again, just inches from the exchange zone. And it looked like this time White had been dealt a knockout blow. She wasn't getting up again, at least not without help.

Meanwhile, Olpe's third and fourth runners made their baton exchange cleanly and suddenly found themselves in the lead.

Frantically, Miller reversed her direction and sprinted back to the beginning of the exchange zone. She plucked the baton from White's outstretched hand and charged forward, in furious pursuit of Olpe's anchor leg.

With her quick ground-gobbling strides, Miller eventually tracked down her target, passed her, and kept right on sprinting to the finish line. By the time she broke the tape, she had opened up a 10-meter lead.

But the drama on the track wasn't over. In trying to hold off Miller's furious charge, the Olpe anchor exhausted herself. Maranatha's Bailey saw her opponent faltering. She mustered her last reserves of energy and unleashed a furious finishing kick. She reeled in the Olpe runner and crossed the finish line in second place. Maranatha had earned four unlikely silver medals. Or so it seemed.

As the various relay teams congratulated and consoled each other, meet officials huddled. They determined that when Miller went back to retrieve the baton from the fallen White, the toe of her purple track spike had crossed the fat white line marking the exchange zone. It was a small infraction, but there would be no grace for the girl named Faith. Pittsburg-St. Mary's was disqualified from the race, and Maranatha, a team with only the eighth-best time going into the meet, was upgraded from runner-up to state champion. Or so it seemed.

Standing on the awards stand several minutes later, the Eagles formed a huddle of their own. They stepped down from their pinnacle, and Ali Bailey, Bethany Zarda, Mallory Keith, and Christa Courtney each found their counterpart from Pittsburg-St. Mary's. Each girl stripped her gold medal from around her neck and pressed it into the hand of a Panther runner. Tears flowed, both on the track and in the stands. No one sobbed harder than White, who had run herself into exhaustion but felt she had cost her three teammates a state championship.

In the days that followed, local media gave more attention to Maranatha's post-race sacrifice than to any of the action that took place on the track. There's just something about people, especially, perhaps, teens, who dare to be different, who dare to redefine cool.

Why? That was the question on every reporter and blogger's mind. Why did four high school runners cut short their moment of

WHY DID FOUR HIGH SCHOOL RUNNERS CUT SHORT THEIR MOMENT OF GLORY AND THEN WILLINGLY GIVE UP WHAT THEY HAD WORKED SO HARD FOR?

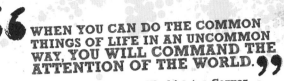

> **WHEN YOU CAN DO THE COMMON THINGS OF LIFE IN AN UNCOMMON WAY, YOU WILL COMMAND THE ATTENTION OF THE WORLD.**
> -George Washington Carver

glory and then willingly give up what they had worked so hard for? Miles upon hot miles of roadwork in the summer. Off-season strength training. Shin splints. Blisters. Sunburn.

And why did they relinquish the gold with no prompting or pressure from parents, youth pastors, coaches, or meet officials? They won fair and square. Yes, the other team's disqualification was unfortunate, but the rules in track and field are clear, and every year, across the country, athletes lose medals due to false starts, dropped relay batons, and assorted other infractions. And there is no epidemic of teen athletes giving up first-place medals once they experience the feeling of that gold resting near their hearts.

Walking the school hallways with a gold medal draped around your neck? Tooling through town with gold dangling from your rearview mirror? That gives you serious "cool points."

But not every teen athlete keeps score the same way as four girls from a small Christian high school in Shawnee, Kansas.

Bailey, a Maranatha senior who will never get another chance for a state championship medal, summed it up this way: "We feel like we ran our hardest, but we did not deserve to win the gold medals. The only right thing to do was to give the girls from Pittsburg-St. Mary's what they deserve."

"It's not about the medals," teammate Zarda agreed. "It's about how you compete and how much you give. If you give it your all, that's all you can ask for."

Daring to swim against the current isn't easy. Especially when it costs you something--like a gold medal. But living by values that Jesus exemplified will do nothing short of revolutionize your life. And probably the lives of those around you. Think about those four shocked St. Mary's Panthers as they received championship medals—and big hugs—from their rivals. Think about the thousands of adults and kids in the stands that day. How many of them will never forget what they saw? How many of them were inspired to be more noble and selfless because of four skinny chicks from suburban Kansas? How many of them had to do a re-boot on their idea of cool?

It's amazing what Jesus can do through people when they have the guts to live life His way. As you know by now, that's what this book is all about. Daring to live by a different set of standards. Daring to live a life that makes a difference.

But how do you make this kind of life happen? How do you value giving in a world that values getting? How do you value mercy in a world that applauds the killer instinct? How do you find a sense of self-worth when you don't have the flawless face or fat bank account of the athletes, rock stars, and movie stars our society celebrates?

It all comes down to which leader you decide to follow.

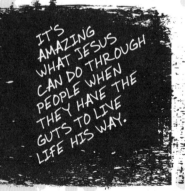

IT'S AMAZING WHAT JESUS CAN DO THROUGH PEOPLE WHEN THEY HAVE THE GUTS TO LIVE LIFE HIS WAY.

### CHECK THIS OUT

Lemmings are small rodents who migrate in huge, furry masses. Sometimes this practice leads to disaster, as one lemming unwittingly follows another as he tumbles off the edge of a cliff or ledge. Multiply this scenario a few dozen times and you have a lot of dead and damaged lemmings.

What's tragic about the plight of lemmings is that some of them eventually realize the danger, but by the time they do, it's too late. They've spent too much time charting their course by focusing on some other creature's backside. They are being moved along against their will by the teeming mass behind them. And good luck getting a crowd of lemmings to change direction once the collective mind has been made up. (Sounds a lot like people, doesn't it?)

Not surprisingly, then, no major sports team is dubbed "The Lemmings." After all, who would want to be named after a critter that foolishly follows its peers, even to its own destruction?

Sadly, many teens today become lemmings in the all-consuming quest to fit in with their peers, to be counted among the ranks of the cool. Thus, anyone wanting to break from the crowd faces the challenge of living by beliefs that others consider uncool, or at least outmoded. After all, how do you take a stand for truth without seeming like, well, a jerk?

This challenge is a tough one, especially when we consider that "cool" is more important than ever––and harder to define than ever. For example, a few years ago Friendster was the social networking site in the United States. It was groundbreaking, revolutionary. It's where all the cool people wanted to be. Hundreds of Friendsters = Hundreds of Cool Points.

Today, Friendster looks like it's wheezing its last dying breaths. It's so uncool that even your grandparents won't use it. It's possible that some of you reading this book haven't even heard of Friendster. That's how fast and how far the cool can fall. Just like a lemming off a cliff.

A game we like to play when we speak to school or church groups is called Cool or Tool?

We'll shout the name of a recording artist, Web site, song, TV show, etc., and ask the group to render their verdicts.

Here are some examples; cast your own vote.

The Jonas Brothers. Cool or tool?

Microsoft...

Yahoo.com...

Stephanie Meyer...

Miley Cyrus...

Oprah Winfrey...

Taylor Swift...

If we were to build a Web site and let all readers of this book cast their votes, you'd realize something when we posted the results: Even among a readership of similar ages and interests, nobody agrees on what cool is. And a lot of people disagree vigorously.

That's why it's foolish and frustrating to let ourselves be imprisoned by the cult of cool. But thank heaven (literally) we have Jesus to bust us out.

## JESUS: SO UNCOOL THAT HE'S ICE COLD

Here's one thing we know about Jesus, the universe's ultimate role model: According to today's cultural standards, Jesus was not, is not, cool. He didn't have popular, influential

> ## ALWAYS DO RIGHT. THIS WILL GRATIFY SOME PEOPLE AND ASTONISH THE REST.
> -Mark Twain

friends. He didn't hail from a cool, happening city. To people in Jesus' day, his hometown of Nazareth was the sticks. Think of the city in your area that everybody makes fun of. You know the one. The ugly, funky-smelling town with the backward people. Their football team sucks, and they don't even have a decent pizza place. That was Nazareth.

Like that wasn't bad enough, Jesus was an outcast even in Nazareth, a lowly Hebrew carpenter weirdo who hung out with the rock-bottom of the social structure. And the rich and powerful, who in reality were not worthy to touch the grimy soles of His sandals, routinely treated Him like trash.

Even when Jesus sparked a burst of adoration from His peers, it didn't last because it was based on what they thought He could do for them. Once, Jesus rode into town on a donkey (not cool!), and people cheered Him like a rock star. But it was because they believed He would help them kick off the restraints of their whacky Roman rulers.

How many from that cheering, palm-branch-waving crowd had His back when He was arrested and put to death? You could count them on one hand--even if you had a bad experience with the band saw in 10th-grade wood shop.

Jesus, though, never got His tunic in a twist about the fickle winds of fame and popularity. His life was never about racking up cool points. It was about helping and serving and listening and teaching and healing.

By not caring one little bit about being cool, Jesus redefined cool. He redefined it by making His life all about giving, not getting. That's why prophecies thousands of years before Jesus' birth proclaimed His greatness. That's why today, 2,000 years after He walked around the countryside with His small band of friends, millions still embrace his teachings.

Let's contrast Jesus with another leader from days gone by. Have you ever heard the name Artaxerxes II? By today's standards, you should have. Good old Arta II ruled the vast kingdom of Persia for about 50 years back around 400 BC. He had 350 wives and hundreds of kids. He oversaw vast building projects. He outfoxed family members who tried to overthrow him. He squashed political revolts like mosquitoes. Through a combination of military might, trickery, and diplomacy, he earned victories over impressive armies from Sparta and Egypt--countries that were the elite varsity when it came to military power.

Conversely, Jesus was dirt-poor. For much of his life, he didn't even have a place to call home. He didn't build palaces or commission sculptures like Arta did. He didn't lead vast armies into battle. His entire life span was much shorter than the time Arta II spent being king.

But who has rocked people's worlds for centuries--and who is an obscure historical footnote? Ever even hear of Artaxerxes II before cracking the pages of this book?

But Jesus is another matter.

All over the world, people risk their lives for Jesus. Like the pirate-radio operator in Iraq who, from a top-secret location, broadcasts Bible teaching throughout the country. If Iraqi fundamentalist

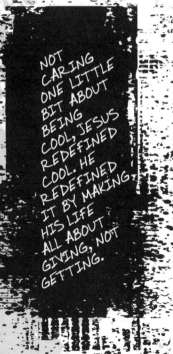

NOT CARING ONE LITTLE BIT ABOUT BEING COOL, JESUS REDEFINED COOL. HE REDEFINED IT BY MAKING HIS LIFE ALL ABOUT GIVING, NOT GETTING.

clerics find him, he's toast.

You don't take a risk like that for someone who is merely cool. A guy who kicked Spartan butt in battle. A guy who built a rockin' palace or two. A guy with a few hundred wives.

That is why Jesus is the ideal model to look to when issues of peer pressure and the "cool factor" hurl themselves at you. Be like Jesus. Jesus never cared for the world's idea of status. He defined greatness to His friends in these words: "Be a servant." Sure, the word "servant" might not sound like a thrilling moniker, but you might be surprised the adventures being a servant can bring. Just ask those four skinny track chicks from Maranatha Academy.

And besides, isn't "servant" a whole lot better than "lemming"?

## GETTING SCHOOLED—AGAIN

Your two friendly To Save A Life authors have been to a high school reunion or two. Okay, or three. (And this doesn't make us uncool. It just makes us older than you. Stuff like needing knee braces to play basketball or tennis and driving minivans with stuffed Garfields suction-cupped to the rear windows—that's what makes us uncool.)

Anyway, we know that most of you reading this book are eons away from a high school reunion, and the subject probably doesn't interest you. That's Okay. It doesn't interest us much either––although it is fun to see chubby middle-aged dudes trying to do the Electric Slide without ripping out the seats of their too-tight Dockers or messing up their comb-overs.

But we did learn a few things at these reunions––things that might help you keep your life right now in perspective. So, imagine yourself 10, 15, or 20 years in the future. You're sucking in your gut and ready to walk into the ballroom of some tired Ramada Inn to see many of your old friends––and rivals––for the first time in years.

Here's what you're likely to discover:

1. Some people age like fine wine. Others age like a carton of milk that fell out of the grocery bag and slid under the backseat of the minivan, where it remained all summer. Look around you next time you're among classmates or the other rookies at your new job. In a few years, many of today's hotties will be "notties." And some of the people who aren't exactly Abercrombie & Fitch models today will turn out to be fit, sharp-looking mature adults. So don't get obsessed with outward appearance. What looks cool has a way of changing.

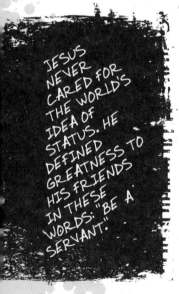

JESUS NEVER CARED FOR THE WORLD'S IDEA OF STATUS. HE DEFINED GREATNESS TO HIS FRIENDS IN THESE WORDS: "BE A SERVANT."

2. The guy or girl who is filling up the trophy case and athletic-records book today might be filling the salad bowl at the Big Country Buffet in a few years. We have gone to school with amazing athletes, marvelous musicians, and thrilling thespians. Unfortunately, many of them never realized success beyond the walls of high school. Why? Because they failed to grasp that graduation is followed by a little thing called The Rest of Your Life. And those who plan to ride the wave of high school

> **NEVER FORGET THAT ONLY DEAD FISH ALWAYS SWIM WITH THE STREAM.**
>
> -Malcolm Muggeridge

cool into the future had better be prepared for a short ride--with an abrupt ending.

**3.** Some of the stuff you think is crucial right now will end up being trivial. You might think that high school reunions are all about re-living the Big Game or reminiscing about how hot Valerie the Vixen looked in her homecoming dress. But we have been surprised at how little story-swapping time was devoted to athletic achievement or grade point averages or awards won. Which brings us to Revelation Number Four.

**4.** True friendships endure. Look around you the next time you're in class, or youth group, or hanging out at your favorite coffee shop. Look at your friends. Many middle-aged people have discovered that their best buds from high school or college are still fulfilling that all-important role. There's just something about the people who are by your side when you endure puberty--and chemistry class. The lesson here? We're not saying you shouldn't strive for success in the classroom, on the athletic field, in the school band, or on the new job. Just don't do it at the expense of your friendships. Because in 10 or 20 years, you might not even remember your GPA or free-throw percentage. But you will remember your true friends.

## A KILLER BOD—NOT WORTH DYING FOR

Writing the section you've just finished (and replaying all those high school reunions in our minds) inspired us to devote a few paragraphs to the subject of physical attractiveness and body image. After all, feeling fat and/or unattractive is one of the top five things that stresses out teens (Seventeen magazine, October 2005).

Additionally, 81 percent of the people who use online dating sites confess to lying about things like their age, height, and weight (Wired magazine, August 2009). Think about that stat for a minute. These are people who consider themselves cool enough to be date-worthy; otherwise they wouldn't be shelling out bucks to sites like Match.com and eHarmony in the first place. And their end-game is to find another flesh-and-blood humanoid to date--at which point the whole illusion about being tall, fit, young, and well-coiffed is going to crumble like a sand castle when the tide comes in.

Still, even though it defies logic, date-hungry dudes and girls lie about themselves. Lies that are so easy to expose.

Here is something that 10, 20, or more years will never change, it seems. The people who think they have hot bods will do all they can to flaunt them. And those who don't will do their best to hide behind clothes, accessories, ridiculous hats—and e-lies. Meanwhile, everybody in between seems to be trying to diet, surgery, or P90X their way into a better, more desirable body.

It's not so tough to figure out why. Everything we see, everywhere we go—the mall, the pool, the multiplex--just about every place but the library, is all about the hard-body hotties. These genetic marvels have been blessed with toned muscles, perfect skin, and digestive systems that apparently burn fat the way a Porsche Turbo Carrera burns high-octane fuel.

And when you aren't looking at these physical wonders in person, they still haunt us, leering at us--and flexing for us--on TV, magazine covers, home pages, and giant billboards. It's intimidating. Sometimes it's downright depressing.

Guys wish, "Why can't I get my abs to pop like that dude's?

And look at those arms--they're bigger than my legs!"

Girls wonder, "Could I ever starve myself enough to get as thin as that woman? And it should be illegal to have legs that long and smooth!"

You may ponder how you can compete with all the buff bods without getting "all swole" yourself. How can you get a date, even get noticed, in the sea of bulging biceps, long legs, and perfect pectorals?

Relax. (Guys: That means stop flexing, okay? You don't need to impress anybody right now, and you're gonna get a cramp if you don't chill. And girls: No need to keep sucking in your gut; you're among friends now.) Before you buy some expensive piece of exercise equipment from a shop-at-home channel or blow hundreds of dollars on questionable nutritional supplements, you need to consider a few facts.

First, those magazine supermodels and media stars you envy aren't as perfect as they look. Posters and photos are retouched, airbrushed, and manipulated in all sorts of ways. (Photoshop is a wondrous thing.) Blemishes and wrinkles are removed. (For that matter, pores are removed!) Flabby arms are made trim; weenie arms are bulked up. And check this-- makeup is used to make guys look like they have washboard abs, when in reality they don't.

And the oils. Let's not forget the oils, which are applied liberally to highlight every sinew, every vein. Sure, you might want to hug these gleaming bods, but they'd probably squirt right out of your arms. (One quick warning to some of you-- and you know who you are: Don't get any ideas about this oil thing. Don't sneak into the kitchen and try to Wesson up your biceps or your legs or your whatever. You're just going to make a mess, stain your clothes, and waste money. Someone in your house needs that oil for cooking, okay?)

Even the people who do look pretty great without all the gimmicks often get their shine on at a high personal cost. For example, steroids pump you up, but they can also alter your personality—not in a good way. They can make you short-tempered and violent. They can make you sterile or even kill you. And don't think that the technically legal supplements (like some of those magic "fat incinerators") are necessarily safer. They have killed teens. And that's not rumor; it's documented fact. You've probably seen some of the news stories. Just because you can find something on the shelves of your local nutrition store endorsed by professional wrestlers doesn't mean it's safe for you to ingest. Getting a killer bod isn't worth risking your life, is it?

Granted, having a hottie body might get you noticed by your crush. But if you want an actual relationship, you must have something more to offer than delicious deltoids and fabulous obliques. After all, gorillas are powerful and physically intimidating, but you don't see them getting lots of dates, do you? (Unless it's with other gorillas, of course.)

CHASING COOL IS LIKE CHASING A SHAPE-SHIFTER. ONE MINUTE YOU'RE TRACKING A ZOMBIE, THE NEXT YOU'RE HOT ON THE TRAIL OF A WOLF.

Once you've captured someone's attention, you're going to need to keep that attention if you want to have a meaningful relationship. You need more than sinew, teeth, and hair. You need a heart that cares, a mind that thinks and wonders, and a soul that reflects Jesus' light. When someone asks your boyfriend or girlfriend what is that magic-cool "something" that sparked the romance between the two of you, do you really want the answer to be, "Well, more than anything else, it was their five percent body fat!"

There's nothing wrong, of course, with wanting to be fit. Your body is a temple, after all, not a Porta-Potty. A balanced diet is a good idea. But a celery stick in each hand is not a balanced meal. The same principle applies to a couple of caffeine-laced protein shakes.

A sensible workout program is a good idea too. But do it for the right reasons. Do it to be healthy, not to be a date magnet. If you want to improve your fitness level, check with a doctor--especially about herbal supplements and their pros and cons. (In other words, don't buy your supps from that hairy gum-chomping guy named Fabiano who wears lots of gold chains and hangs out by the drinking fountain at the gym.)

Finally, keep your fitness goals in perspective. Don't become obsessed with your body image at the expense of your friendships, job, academic career, or life goals. After all, someday your muscles are going to lose some of their size and tone, no matter how hard you try to prevent it. But if you live right, your relationships, your mind, your soul, and your dreams can keep right on growing.

## BRINGING IT HOME

The Bible has this to say about the pointless chase for cool, in all its various forms: "Do not conform any longer to the pattern of this world, but be transformed by the renewing of your mind" (Romans 12:2).

Chasing cool is like chasing a shape-shifter. One minute you're tracking a zombie, the next you're hot on the trail of a wolf. The prey changes forms, and it changes directions. Constantly. Yet everybody keeps chasing. It's as frustrating as trying to do research on dial-up Internet.

We're not going to lie to you: Following Jesus is harder than following something or someone else—or not following anyone. It's harder than just sitting in front of a computer screen and counting and re-counting your Facebook friends.

But when it comes to chasing cool, following Jesus is at least simpler, if not easier.

Here's what we mean by that. We've already talked about getting a grip on the amorphous, shape-shifting concept of pop-culture cool. You'd have better luck roping and corralling a cloud. How many times have you thought you'd "discovered" the funniest clip in the entire history of YouTube—only to learn that all of your friends, and even your friends' bratty little siblings, had already viewed that clip so many times they were already sick of it?

Or, how many times have you started to rave about some hot new indie band, then swallowed your words because the coolest person in your entire circle of friends deems the band lame?

In contrast, following Jesus gives you something to put

your back up against. Something that's not gonna move and leave you tumbling. Something that marks a great place to end this chapter.

1. Let's call this set of eternal and simple (but not easy) rules The Ten Commandments for Living Out the New Cool:

2. Be willing to live like Jesus, even if it means looking different from everyone else.

3. Put others' needs ahead of your own.

4. Serve people; don't demand that they serve you.

5. Speak words of kindness and compassion.

6. When in doubt about saying something, don't. (There's probably an excellent reason behind your hesitation.)

7. Don't do anything because of peer pressure.

8. Pray like there's no tomorrow.

9. Praise people generously, but be a tight-fisted miser with criticism.

10. Be real. All the time.

11. Make your life all about what you can give, not what you can get.

# CHAPTER 3

# DID YOU KNOW?

## THESE PEOPLE ARE LIVING EXAMPLES OF THE "NEW COOL":

- Investor Warren Buffett has given more than $37 billion to various charitable foundations. Meanwhile, he has arranged only a modest inheritance for his own children. He says he believes in giving them "enough so that they feel they could do anything but not so much that they could do nothing."

- At just twenty-three years of age, Leigh Ann Hester, a sergeant in the Kentucky National Guard, earned the Silver Star for exceptional valor. During the Iraq war, she became the first woman to earn the honor, which recognizes "an offensive action against the enemy."

- Real estate magnate Zell Kravinsky has given almost all of his $45 million fortune to health-related charities. But he didn't stop there. After learning that thousands of people die each year while waiting for kidney transplants, he contacted a local hospital and donated one of his kidneys to a stranger.

# 4

Dare 2 Make

# a Difference in Your World

At a high-powered business conference several years ago, an unexpected speaker took center stage to address the large crowd of corporate movers and shakers.

Mister Rogers. Yeah, that Mister Rogers. The guy with the soft voice, the sweater, the sneakers, the songs, and the puppets. (And you might be smirking or rolling your eyes right now, but admit it: You probably grew up with re-runs of the guy's TV show. So don't even try to pretend that you were always too cool for Mister R.)

On the other hand, don't feel too guilty if your first instinct was to dis Mister Fred Rogers. Imagine what that auditorium full of power suits must have thought: I'm here to learn how to monetize my intellectual property-based assets, maximize shareholder value, and shift my emerging-market paradigms—and they bring in the former host of a kiddie show!?

Mister Rogers smiled warmly at his audience. Then, instead of launching into a whiz-bang PowerPoint presentation or fast-paced motivational speech, he offered a gentle request. "Please pause for ten seconds," he said, "to think of the people who have helped you become who you are, those who have cared about you and wanted the best for you in life. Ten seconds. I'll watch the time."

This should have been the cue for people to start checking stock quotes on their PDAs, texting the home office, or maybe leaving the room to make a phone call or smoke a cigarette. But something strange happened instead.

The room got as quiet as a mortuary. Then the silence was broken by a sound not often heard at business conferences—people crying.

Crusty old businessmen sniffled into their red power ties. Ice-queen businesswomen fished in the pockets of their severe gray wool business suits for a tissue. You'd have thought people had just seen the final scene of the saddest movie ever made.

Good old Mister Rogers posed this same question at various events during the later years of his life—including when he earned a Lifetime Achievement award from the Academy of Television Arts and Sciences—and the response was always the same. That's because he understood something about human nature that celebrities and corporate office monkeys in their $1,000 suits just don't get: It's not how much money you make that's truly important in life. It's not your job title. It's not how much you know. It's not the kind of car you drive. It's not the number of search results that pop up when someone Googles your name.

It's the relationships you have with your fellow human beings—especially those who grace your life with friendship, kindness, wise advice, prayers, moral support, open ears, and open arms.

So how about we tackle Mister Rogers' question. Please think about your life for a minute or two. Think about the people who have been there for you, supporting and encouraging you, especially in times of crisis. Think about the friend, sibling, teacher, parent, youth leader, or coach you know you can call on at any time of the day or night. Picture the face of that person who will do anything and everything possible to help you. Recall the words that person spoke to you. Remember that greeting card, note, or e-mail you received. Feel that reassuring arm around your shoulder. Don't skip to the next

**CHAPTER 4:** Dare 2 Make a Difference in Your World

paragraph. Do this instead.

Okay?

Good. Now we can move on. But first, who needs a tissue or at least a shirtsleeve?

If this little exercise helped you be more grateful for some people in your life, that's a good thing. But it's only the beginning of what we want to share with you in this chapter.

As you thought about those angels-on-earth in your life, did you even consider that you are probably an angel-on-earth to someone? And if you are not, you could be. Really. We promise. We'll even show you the way.

## -THE TEST EVERYONE FLUNKED

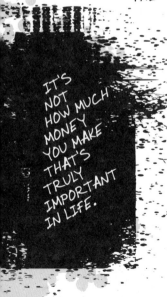

IT'S NOT HOW MUCH MONEY YOU MAKE THAT'S TRULY IMPORTANT IN LIFE.

Recently an East Coast pastor prepared a test for members of his congregation. One Sunday the church ushers worked their way down the aisles giving everyone a sheet of paper. Then the pastor issued a simple challenge: "List the five most powerful, memorable, influential sermons you have heard in your lifetime. You don't need to know the official sermon title, who preached it, or even where you heard it. It might have been on TV, on the Internet, on the radio, or in church. Don't worry too much about the setting. Just write down the basic gist of the message."

How do you think the congregation did with this little test? (If you're a churchgoer,

> ## NO ACT OF KINDNESS, NO MATTER HOW SMALL, IS EVER WASTED.
> —Aesop

how would you do?)

The results? Well, if this were a semester final, everyone would have needed a re-take. A handful of people could name one or two sermons. Someone tried to get by with "The one about God and Jesus and love." One suck-up wrote, "My all-time favorites are your last five sermons, Pastor!"

But no one—in a congregation of hundreds of people—could list five influential sermons. They couldn't list five sermons, period.

The next week, however, everyone did get a re-take. Sort of.

Ushers distributed clean white sheets of paper again. A few in the congregation had to be wondering, What's the preacher man gonna do to make me feel guilty this time around?

Then the new challenge came: "Please number your paper from one to five, just as you did last week. But I don't want a list of sermons today. I want you to list the five people who have had the most profound influence on your life."

How do you think the congregation fared this time?

Yep. They aced the test. And they didn't have to sit there nibbling their pencils, furrowing their brows, and straining their brains to do it, as they had the week before. The names just flowed, along with a few tears.

Many people couldn't stop their list at just five. And most provided more than just a name. They went into detail about the friend who provided a short-term home after the divorce. The mom who came to the hospital every day during the serious illness. The teacher who was a confidant when no one else would listen. The big sister who consistently gave the best advice and always kept a confidence. The youth pastor who always had the time to listen, no matter how large or small the problem or the time of day—or night.

The pastor knew how the whole double-test thing would turn out. He'd done it at his previous church. And while people usually take tests to demonstrate how much they know, these tests were designed to help people discover something. (And no, it's not that sermons are worthless.)

The discovery? People matter. People make a difference. And when we say "people," we mean people just like you.

## LEBRON, OPRAH, OR GATOR THE VOLUNTEER FOOTBALL COACH?

When your humble authors speak around the country, we like to conduct a little test of our own. We ask teens to identify their heroes by listing the five people they admire the most.

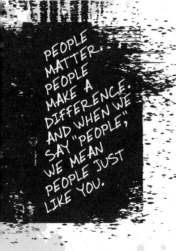

The answers we get during a given year are almost identical to those annual "Most Admired Lists" that you might see on TV, the 'Net, or in your favorite magazine. Every year, pollsters like Harris and Gallup query adults for their "heroes," and the past few polls have featured the usual suspects, including politicians, television personalities, movie stars, musicians, sports stars, etc.

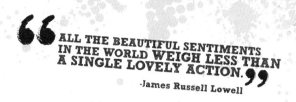

> ALL THE BEAUTIFUL SENTIMENTS
> IN THE WORLD WEIGH LESS THAN
> A SINGLE LOVELY ACTION.
> -James Russell Lowell

In our unofficial teen polls, we see pretty much the same names, with a few other responses sprinkled in. No real surprises.

Then comes Part Two of our test, and we bet you know exactly what's coming. Yep, we change up the question. From "Most Admired" to "Who are the most important people in your life?"

As you might imagine, the lists change completely. Politicians, athletes, and media icons are replaced by grandmas, best friends, big brothers, and journalism teachers. One teen shared this with us: "I play football at my high school, but I am one of the smallest guys on the team. I get knocked around a lot, and I was thinking about quitting. But this guy named Gator, a volunteer football coach, started working with me in the weight room before school. After a couple of weeks, he told me, 'You know, I realize you weigh only a buck-thirty-five, but pound for pound, you are probably the strongest kid in your whole school.'

"Those words gave me so much confidence. My whole attitude about football, and myself, has changed. And I'm going to keep working with Gator until I'm the pound-for-pound strongest guy in the whole conference!"

Wow. Let us pause a moment to say something: Thanks, Gator. Wherever you are. Whatever your real name is. (And even if your real name is, in fact, Gator.)

There's nothing wrong with high-profile heroes. Don't get us wrong. It's great to have someone to look up to, someone who inspires us.

But let's get real. LeBron James is not going to spot you

while you do bench presses every morning before algebra class. Oprah is not going to talk you through the tear-filled aftermath of your break-up with your first serious crush. And your favorite actor is not going to sit in the audience five nights in a row to see you deliver three lines in your high school's production of Meet Me in St. Louis.

It's not the world-famous heroes who do stuff like that. They aren't the ones who make an everyday difference in our lives. It's the everyday heroes like you.

Our informal surveys perfectly mirror similar polls from a variety of sources, such as Yahoo! Answers, MyLot.com, and Answerbag.com. When it comes to answering questions like "Who is the most important person in your life?" and "Which person has had the greatest influence on you?" people invariably respond with one of the following:

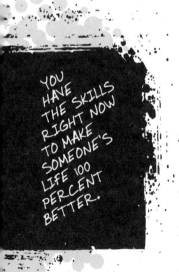

YOU HAVE THE SKILLS RIGHT NOW TO MAKE SOMEONE'S LIFE 100 PERCENT BETTER.

my dad

my mom

my teacher

my BFF

my sweetie

my whole family

my grandparents

my big brother

my coach

my youth leader

my foster parents

Occasionally you'll even see "my dog." But when it gets down to truly personal impact, celebrity sightings are rare.

You see, there's this big bloated myth hovering in the air these days, like one of those giant Thanksgiving Day parade balloons. It's the myth that you have to be famous to do anything truly significant in life. You gotta be rich. You gotta be on TV. You gotta be a rock star. You gotta have at least 1,000 Facebook friends.

You gotta be kidding us! It's time to borrow the neighbor kid's AirSoft gun or your crazy uncle's cross-bow and blast that myth right out of the sky.

You have the skills right now to make someone's life 100 percent better. Probably several people's lives. Bono, as awesome as he is, cannot do for them what you can do.

Now, there's something we want you to read. It's a short poem called "One Solitary Life." Take a minute to read it right now. We'll be waiting for you on the other side.

## ONE SOLITARY LIFE

He was born in an obscure village, the child of a peasant. He grew up in another village, where He worked in a carpenter shop until He was 30. Then, for three years, He was an itinerant preacher.

He never wrote a book. He never held an office. He never had a family or owned a home. He didn't go to college. He never lived in a big city. He never traveled 200 miles from the place where He was born. He did none of the things that usually accompany greatness. He had no credentials but Himself.

He was only 33 when the tide of public opinion turned

against Him. His friends ran away. One of them denied Him. He was turned over to His enemies and went through the mockery of a trial. He was nailed to a cross between two thieves. While He was dying, His executioners gambled for His garments, the only property He had on earth. When He was dead, He was laid in a borrowed grave, through the pity of a friend.

Twenty centuries have come and gone, and today He is the central figure of the human race. I am well within the mark when I say that all the armies that ever marched, all the navies that ever sailed, all the parliaments that ever sat, all the kings that ever reigned—put together—have not affected the life of man on this earth as much as that one, solitary life.*

(*attributed to James Allen Francis)

Welcome back. Good stuff, isn't it? It should be; it's a classic.

## DADDY: THE DIFFERENCE MAKER

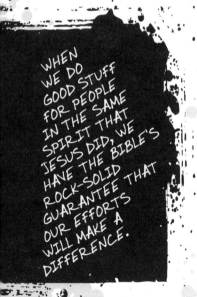

WHEN WE DO GOOD STUFF FOR PEOPLE IN THE SAME SPIRIT THAT JESUS DID, WE HAVE THE BIBLE'S ROCK-SOLID GUARANTEE THAT OUR EFFORTS WILL MAKE A DIFFERENCE.

Toni Morrison is a favorite writer of ours. You might have read some of her stuff in English class. She's won about every major award a writer can win, including the Nobel Prize, the Pulitzer Prize, and the National Book Award, which, in the literary world, is like winning the Super Bowl, capturing the World Series as an encore, then snagging the Stanley Cup just for grins.

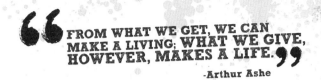

> **FROM WHAT WE GET, WE CAN MAKE A LIVING; WHAT WE GIVE, HOWEVER, MAKES A LIFE.**
>
> -Arthur Ashe

One time she was asked about the key factor in her becoming such a revered author. Her answer surprised a lot of people. "I am a writer today," she said, "because when I was a little girl, my father smiled whenever I entered the room. There is no other reason."

Let's allow those words to sink in. It wasn't Mr. George Wofford's wise career advice that made a difference to his daughter. It wasn't that he sent his little girl to an elite school or used connections in the literary world to score Toni her first book deal. He wasn't able to do those things. He was a small-town Ohio shipyard welder, who for 17 years worked three jobs just to support his family.

But he certainly did do something that made an incredible difference in his daughter's life. He looked up from his newspaper or book when his daughter walked into the room, and he smiled at her with such warm love that it made her feel she could do anything, even become one of the most important writers of her generation. The dedication page of one of Toni's most famous books, Song of Solomon, features a simple one-word tribute: "Daddy." One word that expresses a lifetime of thanks.

That "Daddy's" confidence meant the world to his daughter, even at a young age. When Toni entered elementary school (in first grade), she was the only black child in her grade. But she was also the only child who could read.

What kind of difference will you make in your world? When the people in your life take a 10-second pause to reflect on their difference makers, how cool would it be to have your face, your voice, your kind words come to mind?

What can you do to make that happen? No—let's change

that question: What will you do to make that happen? Don't stress about all that you can't do but wish you could. Because there are so many ways to make another person's life better. And it might just start with something as simple as a smile.

## INSPIRATION TO LIVE BY

*Do all the good you can,*

*By all the means you can,*

*In all the ways you can,*

*In all the places you can,*

*At all the times you can,*

*To all the people you can,*

*As long as ever you can.*

John Wesley

*Nobody makes a greater mistake than he who does nothing be-cause he could only do little.*
Edmund Burke

*A time comes when you need to stop waiting for the man you want to become and start being the man you want to be.*
Bruce Springsteen

*There is more hunger for love and appreciation in this world than for bread.*
Mother Teresa

*From what we get, we can making a living; what we give, however, makes a life.*
Arthur Ashe

*One is not necessarily born with courage, but one is born with potential.*

Maya Angelou

*I will not just live my life.*

*I will not just spend my life.*

*I will invest my life.*

Helen Adams Keller

*The weakest among us has a gift, however seemingly trivial, which is peculiar to him and which worthily used will be a gift also to his race.*

John Ruskin

## FIVE AWESOME THINGS GOD SAYS ABOUT YOU MAKING A DIFFERENCE

1. When you help others, God is pleased. (Hebrews 13:16)

2. When you help others you also help yourself. (Proverbs 11:25)

3. Your words have life-giving power. (Proverbs 18:21)

4. You were created to make a positive difference in the world. (Ephesians 2:10)

5. You are the light of the world. (Matthew 5:14)

# DID YOU KNOW?

*A CELEBRATION OF DIFFERENCE MAKERS, ALL UNDER AGE TWENTY-FIVE*

- Sixteen-year-old Lauren Beeder, who survived cancer as an infant, founded an organization she calls kidsCancervive, which connects young cancer patients with one another via a network of online support groups. For her efforts, she was honored as one of the United States' Most Caring People by the Caring Institute.

- Singer Britt Nicole, whose parents divorced when she was only seven, strives to reach out to others affected by divorce through her songs, speaking opportunities, and other ministry efforts. "My mission statement as an artist," says the twenty-four-year-old, "is to bring healing and restoration to broken people." Despite being a nationally acclaimed artist, Britt works with the youth group at her home church when she is not touring.

- Working from his dorm room at Harvard University, Mark Zuckerberg, nineteen, launched Facebook, a social networking Web site that quickly grew to more than 75 million active users and is now valued at more than $15 billion.

# 5

Dare 2 Know
and Be Known

You could learn a lot from a penguin. At least when it comes to having a sense of community with those around you.

The emperor penguins of Antarctica know the importance of community, teamwork, and togetherness. Their lives depend on it. They huddle together by the hundreds, leaning on their friends and relatives to share the warmth that allows them to survive the brutal, freezing weather their extreme environment affords. Temperatures dip to 70 degrees below zero, and the icy winds can gust up to 100 miles per hour. How cold is that? It can make a sturdy steel screwdriver as brittle as a pretzel stick.

The penguins take turns monitoring the outside of their giant huddle, on the lookout for danger or food. After one of the birds has finished its "perimeter duty," it waddles to the inside of the group so it can get warm and get some sleep. The baby penguins stand on their moms' and dads' feet to protect themselves from the icy surface. If a penguin tried to survive alone, it wouldn't make it through one frozen winter night. But because they stick together, literally, the emperor penguins enjoy a yearly survival rate of better than 95 percent.

Community can equal survival. The proof is in the penguins. And the tougher the conditions, the more important it is for the community to band together. You might not ever need to share physical warmth (unless your school heater goes out this winter), but you can share other types of warmth like encouragement, empathy, ideas, spirituality, and so much more.

For example, you can share the workload on a huge assignment or be part of a study group for finals preparation. And there's something else you can share: the sense of success and accomplishment that results from committed, unselfish teamwork.

The Bible says that a "cord of three strands is not quickly broken" (Ecclesiastes 4:12). Imagine how strong a "cord" of 5, 10, or 50 of you and your friends and family can be. And this principle applies not only to homework, the football field, and the choir risers. It's vital in times of crisis. This truth was brought home to us in a very real way as we completed this book.

## COMMUNITY IN ACTION

Just days before our final writing deadline, Tim, an eighteen-year-old from Todd's church, was hospitalized with a severe sinus infection. Doctors soon discovered that the infection had spread to Tim's brain. He lapsed into a coma, and three short days later, he was gone.

"Tragedy" only begins to describe what Tim's brothers and his single mom faced during Tim's last days. (Tim's father passed away about two years before.) But the tragedy would have been many times worse without the support Tim's family received from their church and school communities.

The moment Tim was admitted to the hospital, his church enlisted a group of volunteers whose task it was to ensure that someone was with the family around the clock. This group provided support in a variety of ways. Seeking information from the hospital staff, going on food runs, praying with Tim's mom and brothers. Making trips to and from the airport as family members from out of state began to arrive.

The support continued after Tim's passing. People brought

food to the home. Friends of Tim's brothers took them out for snacks and a movie, just to help them get their minds off the constant grief. Facebook messages of support and condolence piled up like snowflakes.

Losing a son, a sibling, at such a young age is something no one should have to endure. But imagine going through something like this alone. No support. No comforting hugs. No one to handle the many routine details that have to be done—but seem impossible when you're flailing about in a stormy sea of grief. Community matters.

May none of us need to endure a crisis to realize this truth.

## RUGGED INDIVIDUALISM = RAGGED INDIVIDUALISM

Sadly, some people are reluctant to experience the blessing of being part of a community—the comfort of having others by your side in times of need and the joy of reaching out to others in their times of need.

COMMUNITY CAN EQUAL SURVIVAL. THE PROOF IS IN THE PENGUINS.

The reason? The notion that it's cool to be a lone wolf. "No needs, no obligations for me, thanks. No strings. Don't want to be tied down."

But is it really cool to be a lone wolf? Not according to this pastor we know.

Part of this pastor's duties included visiting residents at one of those "assisted living" centers for senior citizens. (Yeah, an old folks' home.) On his rounds, he met a woman

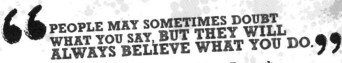

**PEOPLE MAY SOMETIMES DOUBT WHAT YOU SAY, BUT THEY WILL ALWAYS BELIEVE WHAT YOU DO.**

-American Proverb

who brought attention to herself because of her fierce individualism and general contempt for her family, fellow residents, and, especially, the staff at the center. Not surprisingly, the woman never had a guest when the pastor stopped by for a visit.

One week, the pastor found the woman's room empty. A staff member explained that she had passed away a few days previously. But the woman had left word for the pastor. She said she had appreciated his visits so much that she wanted him to officiate at her funeral.

The pastor coordinated the plans for the service with a local funeral home and showed up at the funeral chapel at the appointed time.

He conducted a service that day, but for an audience of only one. And that "one" wasn't breathing. The pastor said later that this was the most memorable funeral he had ever witnessed. But memorable doesn't always mean good.

Here's the problem with lone wolves. They live alone and die alone. What's cool about that?

We hope we've stripped some of the false glamour off the whole Myth of the Rugged Individual, but we know that for many of you, it is not easy to reach out to others—or to allow them to reach out and connect with you.

You'd have to let down your guard. You might have to trust people, and trusting people doesn't come easily for you. You'd have to take a risk.

It's worth the risk. Really.

Here's another real-life story that explains why and how.

## TODD'S STORY, PART TWO

You might not remember the first part of my story, from back at the beginning of the book. To save you the trouble of flipping through a bunch of pages to reread it, here's an eight-word summary of Todd's teen years:

1. alcohol
2. girls
3. street fights
4. guns
5. deception
6. rebellion
7. drugs
8. crime

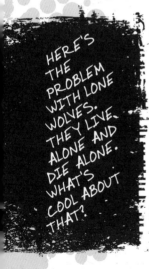

HERE'S THE PROBLEM WITH LONE WOLVES. THEY LIVE ALONE AND DIE ALONE. WHAT'S COOL ABOUT THAT?

Eventually, my wild streak led me right into the interview room of the local sheriff's station, with a gun pointed at me.

You see, a few of my wild friends and I got liquored up one night and decided it would be a good idea to break into a clothing store, then sell the stolen goods at school, making a handsome profit.

We got caught. We got arrested.

One of my buddies sat in custody, screaming at the sheriff, "Take these cuffs offa me, and I'll kick your ***." I sat there thinking, I wonder how my dad, the prominent local pastor, is going to take this news?

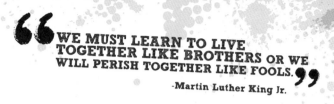

A bit of perspective is in order here: I grew up in a small town of about 3,000 people. Everybody in town knew my dad. He pastored one of the more prominent churches in the area, and he also had his own show on the local radio station. He was also six-foot-two, 285 pounds—a former semi-pro football player and champion power-lifter. Kinda hard to miss.

And now his honor-student, four-sport varsity athlete son was a criminal. Hey, it was front-page news in our local paper when our town got its first stop light. You can imagine how this particular crime story was about to play out.

I should also mention that my dad is a loud, off-the-charts extrovert, while I was such an introvert that I used to see if I could make it through entire days without uttering a single word. One reason I started drinking hard liquor at the ripe old age of twelve is that I didn't think I would be able to even say hello to a girl without a few shots of liquid courage in me.

Additionally, I fancied myself such a rugged individualist that I insisted that my bedroom had to be separate from our official house. I set up my space in the back of the detached garage (and, later, the storage shed). I was way too cool and aloof to share the same roof with the rest of my family.

I look at the title of this chapter, "Dare 2 Know and Be Known," and I have to laugh. I know a little bit about the struggles of "being known."

Anyway, my brief stint as a criminal eventually landed me in a packed courtroom, where my fellow inept law-breakers and I escaped with (mercifully) suspended sentences and probation. But the whole thing was humiliating. My modest accomplishments in the classroom and the athletic arena had escaped much of the community's knowledge, but everybody knew about this.

I felt awful for my family, especially my dad. I was afraid people would start leaving his church because of me. So I came up with a plan. I would move from Wyoming to California to live with my uncle. I was dead serious about this. I was an embarrassment to my family, and the only solution was to remove the source of that embarrassment. Me.

If this plan didn't go over well with the family, I had a back-up: I would pull all my money out of savings and run away—simply disappear. Sounds pretty daring, doesn't it?

I wish I could say that my desire to flee was completely altruistic, but that would be a lie. I wanted to protect myself too. From the gossip. The whispers. The disapproving stares. More hallway lectures from "shocked and disappointed" teachers.

So, I sat the family down and laid out my plan. I really thought everyone would go for it. Especially my brother Chadd, with whom I had regular fistfights that were so spectacular we should have charged admission.

I was shocked at their response.

They begged me to stay. In fact, they said that if the church or the town in general couldn't forgive me for my mistake, we'd move.

Please understand, I don't come from one of those TV Land families. My relationship with my parents was strained, to say the least. I sure couldn't whup my dad, but I did what I could to get under his skin. For example, I'd starve myself so I could wrestle at the lowest possible weight class, even though it wreaked havoc on my health and drove him absolutely mad bat crazy with rage. I brawled with two of my three brothers. Most of the time, I was a jerk. I'm surprised the family dog would even put up with me.

But these people stuck by me at the most humiliating point of my life. They supported me without a moment's hesitation.

The same thing happened at church. And at school. In the To Save A Life movie, sports star Jake starts reaching out to disenfranchised kids at his school. A kid named Tim at my school did that for me. We became best friends. And he became a bridge for establishing new friendships for me.

When the local Big Brothers chapter had a budding young criminal who needed some guidance, they came to me and gave me a chance to redeem myself. The school guidance counselor asked me to present my story to various student groups, as a cautionary tale. Another chance to win back the respect I had thrown away.

The homecoming queen befriended me—and eventually became my girlfriend.

Finally, I got a semi-regular gig speaking to groups of "Talented and Gifted, but At-Risk" teens. (I'm still not sure about the "talented and gifted" part. But at-risk? Yeah, I get that.)

I want to be real with you. This whole thing didn't turn out like a Disney film. There was gossip. There were cheapshots from fellow students. There were parents who wouldn't let their daughters date me. (To be fair, that was probably prudent on their part, for many, many reasons.)

But, in general, the community rallied around me, and I would not have been able to cope without their support. People reached out to me, and it set the course for my life. That's why I'm typing these words right now.

We're all in this together. And together is the only way we're going to make it.

## COMM NITY: WHAT'S MISSING?

If you remember only one sentence from Todd's story, let it be this: We're all in this together. God designed people to function best as a team. That's why we have different strengths—and different weaknesses. Think of your family, your community, or your church as a body. Different parts, different functions. But every part is needed for things to function optimally.

In today's world, many parts of the Body are injured, tired, or feeling unappreciated. Maybe this describes you. At times like these, we need to reach out to others and allow them to reach out to us. Those of you who are basket-ball players (like Todd) know what you do when you dislocate a finger in the middle of a big game: You tape the injured finger to a healthy, strong finger. For the support. For the strength. For the protection. It's no accident that this procedure is called buddy taping.

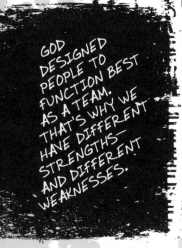

GOD DESIGNED PEOPLE TO FUNCTION BEST AS A TEAM. THAT'S WHY WE HAVE DIFFERENT STRENGTHS—AND DIFFERENT WEAKNESSES.

Everyone needs a buddy.

Who might you need to be buddy taped to and who might need to be buddy taped to you?

At the end of this book, you will find some blank pages entitled How I Can Make a Difference. This is not an accident. We want you to use these pages.

> ## FOR A COMMUNITY TO BE WHOLE AND HEALTHY, IT MUST BE BASED ON PEOPLE'S LOVE AND CONCERN FOR EACH OTHER.
>
> -Millard Fuller, founder of Habitat for Humanity

Here's how:

1. Ask God to show you someone (or several someones) in your life who has a need. Maybe that person needs a friend, a confidant, a prayer partner, or just a ride to school. It could be that God will bring someone to your mind—or your Facebook page—and you won't know right away what the need is. You might have to reach out to find the answer. That's where it begins— with a willingness to be the help someone needs.

2. Write down the name or names in this book. Make things tangible.

3. List some ways you might be able to help. Be specific. Be creative. Be prayerful.

4. Call in reinforcements, if needed. You might find that a person God has brought to mind is dealing with a significant, industrial-strength problem. If you feel like you're in over your head, get extra help. The back of this book also offers a great list of resources for a variety of challenges, from eating disorders to self-abuse to depression to suicide prevention.

We know that for some of you reading this book, life sucks. The idea of helping someone else seems beyond the call of duty. But your life will suck less if you reach out to someone in trouble. God will give you the strength to help. He'll show you where to find answers. And you might even find healing for yourself in the process of helping someone else. God has a way of making that happen.

One final request: Please let us know how this book has impacted you and your friends. And tell us about your story. You can post your message on Facebook.com/ToSaveALife or Twitter.com/ToSaveALife.

# CHAPTER 5

# DID YOU KNOW?

Who we choose, and who we refuse, to hang with says a lot about who we are-or how we see ourselves. Ask yourself, "What's the biggest turn-off for me when I first meet someone?" Then ask yourself, "What does this say about me?"

For instance:

• Do people who grab the spotlight make you crazy? (Maybe you like to be the center of attention.)

• Do you shy away from shy people? (Maybe you're uncomfortable with silence and feel it's your responsibility to fill it with chatter.)

• Do you pretend not to see people who are physically or mentally challenged? (Maybe you're so afraid of saying or doing something wrong that it's easier to do nothing at all.)

Do know-it-alls make you squirm? (Maybe you don't really recognize what an amazing person you are.)

WAYS THAT I CAN MAKE A DIFFERENCE IN MY WORLD AND IN MY SCHOOL?

_____
_____
_____
_____
_____
_____
_____
_____
_____
_____
_____
_____
_____
_____
_____
_____
_____
_____
_____
_____
_____
_____
_____
_____
_____

## RESOURCES

Life isn't always easy; we often need the help of others. You may have experienced challenges in your own life, or maybe your friends, family, or teens you work with have. There are places to find real-life help with tough circumstances. Start with family, friends, church, counselors, and teachers. If you don't have someone you can talk to, check out some of the resources and partners on this page that may be helpful. If you're feeling desperate or afraid, reach out to someone today.

## DEALING WITH THE TOUGH STUFF

If you are in crisis, need immediate help, or are facing a potentially life-threatening emergency, call 911 immediately.

## SUICIDE:

National Suicide Prevention Hotline – suicidepreventionlifeline.org

If you or someone you know is considering suicide, do not wait to get help. Take the concern seriously and call 1-800-273-TALK to talk to someone who cares.

The Hopeline – thehopeline.com

Offers help to teens who are struggling with critical life issues and who may be considering self-harm or suicide. Call 1-800-394-HOPE to talk with a Hope Coach, or communicate by chat or text.

## SELF-INJURY:

To Write Love on Her Arms – twloha.org

You were created to love and be loved. Your life matters.

TWLOHA is a movement dedicated to hope and finding help for people struggling with depression, addiction, self-injury, and suicide.

S.A.F.E. – selfinjury.com

S.A.F.E. ALTERNATIVES is a nationally recognized treatment approach, professional network, and educational resource base committed to helping you and others end self-abusive behavior.

## SUBSTANCE ABUSE:

Teen Challenge – teenchallengeusa.com

Faith-based help and healing for those facing drug addiction and life-controlling problems. Teen Challenge has centers located in 70 different countries.

## DEPRESSION:

American Medical Association's Essential Guide to Depression – www.ama-assn.org

A guide featuring solid, non-technical wording info on depression and mood disorders.

For Doing the Right Thing:

Rachel's Challenge – rachelschallenge.com

The largest public high school assembly program in the country creating a chain reaction of kindness and compassion.

Challenge Day – challengeday.org

A program working toward schools where every student feels safe, loved, and celebrated.

"I have this theory that if one person can go out of their way to show compassion, then it will start a chain reaction of the same. People will never know how far a little kindness can go."
Rachel Joy Scott

## MISSION:

Inspire, equip and empower students and adults to prevent bullying, violence and suicides while creating a permanent positive culture change in their schools, businesses and communities by starting a chain reaction of kindness and compassion patterned after the life and writings of Rachel Joy Scott, the first victim in the Columbine High School shootings.

Rachel's story dramatically illustrates how deliberately reaching out to others with kind words and little acts of kindness can have a life-changing impact. It is a powerful antidote to bullying and violence, and is a real deterrent to suicide. **Inspired by her journals, essays and othewritings, we spread her message of hope and action worldwide through powerful educational and corporate presentations.**

## OBJECTIVES:

**Rachel's Challenge is the only integrated Kindergarten-through-Corporate program of its kind and is uniquely positioned to inspire, equip and empower students at every level to make a difference in their world by:**

Creating a safe learning environment by re-establishing civility and delivering proactive antidotes to violence, bullying and suicide.

Improving achievement by engaging heart, head and hands in the learning process.

Providing social/emotional education that is both color-blind and culturally relevant.

Training adults to inspire, equip and empower students of all ages to affect permanent positive change in themselves, their school and the community.

## REACH AND IMPACT:

1.3 million students in more than 1,300 schools and businesses annually

Hundreds of suicides averted every year – over 290 in the past 18 months

Districts report 80%-90% reductions in disciplinary referrals and suspensions

At least 7 school shootings averted since 2005

For more information about Rachel's Challenge and our programs, contact us at 877.895.7060 or visit our website at www.rachelschallenge.org.

## YOU MAY JUST START A CHAIN REACTION.

Bring the Biggest Faith Based Film of the Year to your bookstore! *To Save A Life* is coming on DVD for home use this August. **>>**

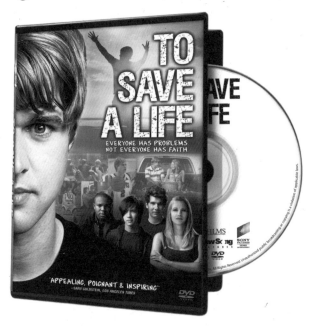

## The home-use DVD includes these special features:

+ Deleted Scenes
+ Music Videos ("Bounce" by J-Rus & "Sunset Cliffs" by Paul Wright)
+ Commentary
+ Gag reel
+ Behind the Scenes feature

*NOTE: To Save A Life is rated PG-13 for realistic topics that may not be suitable for younger viewers.*

# Dare to be Inspired...by these *To Save A Life* Books.

### To Save A Life novel
Based on the screenplay of the movie and featuring additional scenes and back stories not shown in the film.
ISBN: 978-0-9823-7446-7
**$14.99 SRP**

### Life Saver: The Ultimate Devotional Handbook for Teens
Features 52 topics to help young people grow in their faith and share God's love with others.
ISBN: 978-1-9355-4121-9
**$12.99 SRP**

### To Save A Life: Dare to Make Your Life Count
A powerful, inspirational book that challenges teens to apply the principles of the movie by identifying with Jesus and befriending those who are lost, left out, hurting and lonely.
ISBN: 978-1-9355-4106-6
**$12.99 SRP**

Look for these books at your local Christian bookstore or visit **Outreach.com** for bulk quantities.